Our Faerie Best

Our Faerie Best

from the pages of FATE magazine

selected by the editors of FATE

2011
Galde Press
Lakeville, Minnesota, U.S.A.

Our Faerie Best

Printed in the United States of America

First Edition
Second Printing, 2011

Cover painting by Beth Hansen

Galde Press
PO Box 460
Lakeville, Minnesota 55044–0460

Contents

Could Fairies Be Real?

Paul M. Vest, Ph.D.
October 1951

We realize that in this day of the H-Bomb and supersonic aircraft, the world of fairies and nature sprites belong to a mellower period of civilization when people had time to ponder on the simpler phases of life. Today no one wants to appear gullible. We want to think we "know all the answers." Undoubtedly this attitude of mind makes for material success but may it not lead us to miss other far more significant advances in human thought?

The writer is going to make no attempt to prove the actual existence of fairies or to offer any plea for the authenticity of the famous Cottingley photographs, copies of which accompany this article. We merely present herewith the facts of the case and leave it up to each reader individually to decide for himself whether or not the photographs are genuine or false.

If they are genuine, then the world-old belief in fairies has its basis in reality. In which case here on our own planet may exist thousands of tiny creatures who lead a wonderful objective existence of their own separated from the world of mortals only by a slight variation in vibration.

In every land and in nearly every period of civilization we find reports of fairies. In Ireland, accounts of the "little people" have always been taken seriously; in Germany many believe in the undines, salamanders, and gnomes; native Polynesians hold in great awe the "Mennehunies" (little men) (See Max Freedom Long's "Secret Science Behind Miracles"). And for centuries England has had its many "true" stories of dryads, forest nymphs, and fairies who dance down moonbeams.

Those who believed they had actually seen the fairies remained unshaken in their convictions, but most other people were inclined to doubt such tales. Then in 1920 in the December issue of *Strand Magazine* in London there appeared several purportedly authentic photographs of fairies. The pictures were said to have been taken by two girls with a cheap camera. The appearance of the photographs immediately stirred up a considerable furor in England. At first the cry of "Fake!" was heard, but as the true facts of the story came out many were convinced.

A number of writers and scientists became interested in the pictures. Among them was Sir Arthur Conan Doyle. He secured the negatives and took them to one of England's eminent photographic experts, Mr. A. Snelling, who for over thirty years had been allied with the Autotype Company and Illingsworth's Photographic Laboratories. Snelling laughed at the thought that even an expert could fool him with a faked photograph. Of course he was rather skeptical at first about the "fairy" pictures, but after exhaustive tests of the negatives, he made public the statement that he was willing to risk his professional reputation in asserting that

Frances and leaping fairy. Photo taken by Elsie with Cameo camera ostensibly shows motion according to the experts.

"(1) The photographs were single exposures. (2) All figures of the fairies had actually moved during the exposure which was 'instantaneous.'" He further stated in his report that he could discover not the slightest evidence of "faking" in the fairy pictures and he was willing to go on record as having so stated.

Still not content, Doyle took the negatives to the Kodak Company's offices in Kingsway. There, experts of the company made a minute examination of the plates. Neither of them could find any evidence of "trick" photography or "tampering." They would not, however, go on public record as swearing the plates were actual photographs of fairies. They merely stated emphatically that they could "find no flaw in the negatives."

Following this, enlargements were made and exhaustively studied by many other photographic experts both in England and in the U.S., but not one could prove that the plates were not genuine. One expert at the

Illingsworth Company was of the opinion that "rather similar" photographs might be produced by very clever studio painting, but the highly significant fact remained that the figures in the Cottingley photographs had actually been in motion when photographed.

Now that we have the opinions of experts to whom Sir Arthur showed the negatives, let us consider the circumstances under which the pictures were taken. In the *Westminster Gazette* of January 12, 1921, we find an article written by a special reporter sent to Cottingley to get the facts. Following are excerpts from his report:

DO FAIRIES EXIST?
INVESTIGATION IN A
YORKSHIRE VALLEY
COTTINGLEY'S MYSTERY
STORY OF THE GIRL WHO
TOOK THE SNAPSHOTS

"...My mission to Yorkshire was to secure evidence, if possible, which would prove or disprove the claim that fairies existed. I frankly confess that I failed.

"The particular fairyland is a picturesque little spot off the beaten track two or three miles from Bingley. Here is a small village called Cottingley, almost hidden in a break in the upland, through which tumbles a tiny stream, known as Cottingley Beck, on its way to the Aire, less than a mile away. The 'heroine' of Sir Conan Doyle's story is Miss Elsie Wright who resides with her parents at 31 Lynwood Terrace. The little stream runs past the back of the house and the photographs were taken not more than a hundred yards away. When Miss Wright made the acquaintance of the fairies she was accompanied by her cousin, Frances Griffiths, who resides at Dean Road, Scarborough.

"One photograph taken by Miss Wright in the summer of 1917, when she was 16, shows her cousin, then a child of 10, with a group of four fairies dancing in the air before her, and in the other, taken some months afterwards, Elsie, seated on the grass, has a quaint gnome dancing beside her.

"There are certain facts which stand out clearly and which none of the evidence I was able to obtain could shake. No other people have seen the fairies, though everybody in the little village knew of their alleged existence; when Elsie took the photograph she was unacquainted with the use of a camera, and succeeded at the first attempt; the girls did not invite a third person to see the wonderful visitors and no attempt was made to make the discovery public.

"First, I interviewed Mrs. Wright who, without hesitation, narrated the whole of the circumstances without adding any comment. The girls, she said, would spend the whole of the day in the narrow valley, even taking their lunch with them, though they were within a stone's throw of the house. Elsie was not robust and did not work during the summer months, so that she could derive as much benefit as possible from playing in the open. She had often talked about seeing the fairies, but her parents considered it was nothing more than childish fancy and let it pass.

"Mr. Wright came into possession of a small camera in 1917 and one Saturday afternoon yielded to the persistent entreaties of his daughter and allowed her to take it out. He placed one plate in position and explained to her how to take a 'snap.' The children went away in high glee and returned in less than an hour, requesting Mr. Wright to develop the plate. While this was being done Elsie noticed that the fairies were beginning to show, and exclaimed in an excited tone to her cousin, 'Oh, Frances, the fairies are on the plate!' The second photograph was equally successful, and a few prints from each plate were given to friends as curiosities about a year ago. They evidently attracted little notice until one was shown to some of the delegates at a Theosophical Congress in Harrogate last summer.

"Mrs. Wright certainly gave me the impression that she had no desire to keep anything back, and answered my questions quite frankly. She told me that Elsie had always been a truthful girl and there were neighbors who accepted the story of the fairies simply on the strength of their knowledge of her....

"At that time her father knew little of photography, 'only what he had picked up by dodging about with the camera,' as he put it.

"When he came home from the neighbouring mill and was told the nature of my errand, he said he was 'fed up' with the whole business and had nothing else to tell. However, he detailed the story I had already heard from his wife, agreeing in every particular, and Elsie's account given to me in Bradford, added nothing new.

"Thus I had the information from the three members of the family at different times and without variation. The parents confessed they had some difficulty in accepting the photographs as genuine and even questioned the children as to how they faked them. The children persisted in their story and denied any act of dishonesty. Then they 'let it go at that.' Even now their belief in the existence of the fairies is merely an acceptance of the statements of their daughter and her cousin.

"Elsie is a tall, slim girl, with a wealth of auburn hair, through which a narrow gold band, circling her head, was entwined.

"Like her parents, she just said she had nothing to say about the photographs and, singularly enough, used the same expression as her father and mother—'I am "fed up" with the thing.'

"She gradually became communicative, however, and told me how she came to take the first photograph.

"Asked where the fairies came from, she replied that she did not know.

" 'Did you see them come?' I asked; and on receiving an affirmative reply, suggested that she must have noticed where they came from.

"Miss Wright hesitated, and laughingly answered, 'I can't say.' She was equally at a loss to explain where they went after dancing near her, and was embarrassed when I pressed for a fuller explanation.

"When she had been with her cousin she had often seen them before. They were only kiddies when they first saw them, she remarked, and did not tell anybody.

Fairy offering flowers to Elsie. She said dress was pink, wings yellowish.

"'But,' I went on, 'it is natural to expect that a child seeing fairies for the first time, would tell its mother.' Her answer was to repeat that she did not tell anybody. The first occasion on which fairies were seen, it transpired, was in 1915.

"In reply to further questions, Miss Wright said she had seen them since, and had photographed them, and the plates were in the possession of Mr. Gardner (President, Theosophical Society). Even after several prints of the first lot of fairies had been given to friends, she did not inform anybody that she had seen them again. The fact that nobody else in the village had seen them gave her no surprise. She firmly believed that she and her cousin were the only persons who had been so fortunate, and was equally convinced that nobody else would be. 'If anybody else were there,' she said, 'the fairies would not come out.'

"Further questions put with the object of eliciting a reason for that statement were only answered with smiles and a final significant remark, 'You don't understand.'"

Thus we; have the story of the Cottingley photographs as related by an unbiased newspaper reporter.

Surely it would have been to his advantage as a member of the press, to have shown up the entire affair as a fraud if there had been the slightest evidence to have warranted his attempting to do so. It is true that several critics, without bothering to make a personal investigation, have made bitter newspaper attacks upon the girls and their families. But no shred of proof was ever unearthed to brand either the photographs or the accounts of Elsie and Frances as false in any way.

In fact, as the story spread throughout the British Isles, reports came in from honest and reliable persons who swore that they too had seen the "little people." Many declared that they had heretofore feared to mention what they saw since people might consider them crazy.

Halliwell Sutcliffe, the novelist, wrote that his close friend, a reputable schoolmaster whose word was beyond question, had often told him of playing with fairies in the meadows near his home.

Even from faraway Australia, Africa, and Greenland came letters from persons who were willing to swear they too had seen fairies.

Later, several more expensive cameras were given to the girls by Mr. Gardner and additional photographs were taken by Elsie and Frances in Cottingley Glen. The fairies appeared on a number of the plates.

A man considered by both E. L. Gardner and Sir Conan Doyle to be one of England's most gifted clairvoyants was taken to the Glen to verify the girls' accounts. In writing of this occasion, Sir Conan Doyle says, "Mr. Gardner had a friend, whom I will call Mr. Sergeant, who held a commission in the Tank Corps in the war and is an honourable gentleman with neither the will to deceive nor any conceivable object in doing so. This gentleman had the enviable gift of clairvoyance in a very high degree, and it occurred to Mr. Gardner that we might use him as a check upon the statements of the girls.

Elsie and gnome. Picture taken by Frances with Mr. Wright's "Midge" camera.

"I have before me his reports, which are in the form of notes made as he actually watched the phenomena recorded. Seated with the girls he saw all that they saw and more, for his powers proved to be considerably greater.

Having distinguished a psychic object, he would point in the direction and ask them for a description, which he always obtained correctly. The whole glen, according to his account, was swarming with many forms of elemental life, and he saw not only wood-elves, gnomes, and goblins, but the rarer undines, floating over the stream."

Sergeant, however, was not able to give to the fairies sufficient objective visibility on the physical plane to capture their images on a photographic plate. Apparently Elsie and Frances are the only persons ever known to have possessed this strange ability.

In summing up his report on the affair, Sir Conan Doyle said, "I do not myself contend that the proof is as overwhelming as in the case of spiritualistic phenomena. We cannot call upon the brightest brains in the scientific world, the Crookes, the Lodges, or the Lombrosos, for confirmation. But that also may come and, for the present, while more evidence will be welcome, there is enough already convincing evidence available."

These are the true facts of the Cottingley photographs so far as they are known. But as to whether or not fairies really do exist, perhaps we shall have to leave the mystery unsolved until science develops instruments with which we may look into new vibrational dimensions ordinarily invisible to the human eye.

Fairies Were Real

Evidence indicates that fairies did exist —that they built homes, raised crops and intermarried.

Virginia Stumbough
November 1957

Peter Pan was right. Fairies did live. They were among our remote ancestors, actually the last of the Neolithic peoples in Europe. They were dominant in England for only 500 years and had disappeared in Europe, as a pure race, by the end of the Middle Ages.

These short, stocky, dark-skinned people came from the region of the Mediterranean over 5,000 years ago. Among the last places these legendary folk lived were hidden villages in isolated, northern areas of Wales, Cornwall, the Scottish Highlands, Ireland, upper Brittany, the Isle of Man, and Lapland. We still can walk their faint tracks today, along the length of the Long Mynd hilltop in Shropshire, England, or along the barely visible path from the banks of the Humber River south through Burton Stather and down towards Risby Warren above the winding Trent. These are the "oldest roads in Britain" according to Henry Treece's article in *Everybody's Magazine.*

We have been taught to think of fairies as gossamer, minute creatures of our imaginations, delightful and amusing, but intended only for children's stories.

But fairies were real. They lived in houses and villages with their own herds, priests, kings, and queens. They were a people apart who eventually intermarried with other peoples and finally could not be distinguished from them. By today's standards they were odd—but they were never supernormal.

Yet superstitions and stories handed down by word of mouth from one generation to the next finally changed them from historic peoples into dancing shadows.

Shakespeare, in his *Midsummer Night's Dream*, was largely responsible for turning fairies into phantoms. All the Elizabethan writers spoke of them as real people, says M. W. Latham in *The Elizabethan Fairies.* Robert Kirk, an Englishman writing in 1691, said that fairies were "no Nonentities or Phantasms, Creatures proceeding from an affrighted apprehensione, confused or crazed Sense, but Realities, appearing to a stable Man in his awaking Sense, and enduring a rational Tryall of their Being."

Fairies, everyone agreed, were human, dwelt in knolls and below ground, could appear and disappear at will, and felt natural hunger, grief, passions, and vexations. Thomas Heywood's *Hierarchie* asserted that they did "eat, drinke, sit at table, talke and discourse after the manner of our fellowes; so that they may be easily took for some friend or acquaintance." But though the folk of all countries continued to know them as live beings the church, for reasons of its own, denounced them as spirits and myths and, with William Shakespeare, helped change them into what they never were.

Fairies practiced the witch cult or Old Religion of ancient times, from which so many of the modern rituals, folk practices and beliefs have stemmed, says Dr. Margaret Murray in *The God of the Witches.* Henry Treece points out that these people inhabited Europe before the coming of the Aryans and Celts to England and brought with them a knowledge of settled homes, and the growing of barley to carry them through the barren winter months.

Their basic god was naturally the soil, Mother Earth, who gave them food and the flint for their hunting knives. They worshipped her at sowing time with blood sacrifice, to fertilize the earth. But, as Dr. Murray describes in detail, many facets of their religion were abhorrent to the church: gods of evil as well as good, plural marriages, midnight dancing and sexual orgies, the wearing of masks and other secrecies.

What no one realized, says Dr. Murray, was that these people were practicing ancient and honored fertility rites. And only by retreating before the advance of civilized man were the fairy folk able to keep their old customs, totems, and festivals intact. As life around them changed from the old ways the fairy folk seemed less and less real. They remained untouched in their hidden meadows, chalk-hill villages, and long burial burrows. For hundreds of years they kept themselves hidden and thus faded into folklore.

Many prominent people of the Middle Ages were said by their contemporaries to have contact with the fairies. Conn, King of Tara in Ireland, married a fairy for his second wife. Andro Man, of Aberdeen, Scotland, married the Queen of Elphan, lived with her for thirty-two years during which time they had several children. Sieur de Bourlemont, who owned the fairy tree around which Joan of Arc was said to dance, also had a fairy wife. James I of Scotland helped burn witches for haunting and dealing with the fairies. James VI of Scotland alternately referred to the fairies as "our good neighbors" and "spirits of the devil."

In Ireland, where still today many folk swear they have seen the Little People, where leprechauns may live in any hill, the fairies were called Tuatha. The Milesians, Bronze Age peoples who invaded Ireland from Spain 3,000 years ago, tried to exterminate them but learned to live in peace. The name for Puck, Pwcca, is today the same in Wales as in Ireland. Their spread to Brittany in France is easily understood, for it was closely tied by trade and colonization to Wales and Cornwall, where fairies lived later than in other areas of Britain. Even today the peoples of Wales and Brittany find many similarities in their language.

The fairies were cattlemen, living on and with animals, with a cattle economy and superior powers as horse breeders. Treece tells how, as their lands were finally taken over by other cultures, such as that of the "giants," the tall, fair Aryans, the fairies retreated to swamps and islands.

Several peoples living today can give us some idea of what the fairies must have been like, according to Dr. Murray. They lived much like the Kurumbas tribes in the Neilgherry Hills of South India. Like the Bedouins of Asia and the Gypsies of Europe, they intermarried and were gradually absorbed by villagers in the rural and forest districts of Britain, Brittany, western France, and Germany, where they lived.

The original dwarf inhabitants of Scandinavia were fairies. The fairies disappeared first as a race in England, in Scotland they were gone by the end of the sixteenth century, and by the end of the eighteenth century they were gone everywhere. But their story will live for as long as men tell stories.

We think of fairies as being an inch or two tall, with transparent wings, but according to Margaret Murray, they were of human size, but shorter than average. The men were about five-feet five-inches tall, and the women were smaller.

Ann Page, in Shakespeare's *Merry Wives of Windsor,* dressed as a fairy and expected to be taken for one, though she was of normal size. Medieval plays often had fairy characters, usually played by boys since men were too large, children too small, and women did not act on the stage. Alpine fairies are described as shorter and stouter than men, as dwarfs. Fairies often were mistaken for villagers since they dressed and acted like other people when they went among them.

It is not hard, once we accept the premise that fairies were real, says Latham, to find many details about their appearance and habits. In Elizabethan times Good Queen Bess was often said to be as beautiful as a fairy. Apparently this was considered to be a high complement. Evidently many fairy women had extraordinary beauty. We don't think of today's Laplanders, whom they are said to resemble, as being beautiful with their dark skins and short stature, yet the literature and drawings of the time portrayed them as most attractive. Their hair was long and silky when they were young; they took great pride in keeping it clean and well combed. The only manner of their dress consistently the same in all lands, for all periods, was the green color of their clothes and the fact that they always wore hats. These hats or caps were of different styles, but of such major importance that a fairy would risk capture or pay ransom to recover his cap when it was lost.

In West Highland fairies wore green, conical caps like those of the Swedish Lapps today; in Ireland they wore gray coats and stockings and black wool caps; Welshmen wore red-tripled caps, and ladies, tall waving hats; on the Isle of Man the fairies wore undyed woolen clothes and pointed, red caps; in Upper Brittany their caps were like crowns, in Hildesheim fairies dressed like peasants but always wore hoods; the Slav fairies wore short waistcoats, tight pants, and three-cornered hats.

The homespun wool of their clothing varied according to tribe and rank. It was undyed or was dyed dark green or blue. Green was a favorite color because it blended with the trees and fields furnishing camouflage for hunting or being hunted. The dark blue color looked black and fairies were often referred to as black fairies, partly because of this, partly because of their dark complexions and habit of blackening their faces as part of their religious rituals, according to Dr. Murray.

European fairies and the peris and Yakshas of Arabia, Persia, and India were beautiful, sweet, and gentle. The fairies who entertained at Apthorp for Queen Anne of Denmark were spoken of as blessed and good. In Bavaria fairy women were said to be modest, shy, and retiring in nature. All fairy folk liked solitude. They were merry and capricious, however, loving to play practical jokes. One weakness of fairy women was their liking for men, fairy or otherwise. They loved to cook and bake, and delighted in cleanliness, washing, and bathing frequently. Medieval manuscripts report that they could "spine, dy, and embroyder." Strangely enough, they had spindles but no spinning wheels or looms. They never acquired the art of making looms, but borrowed or stole them from the villagers for their weaving.

Fairies never lived singly but always in groups as if for mutual help and protection. They spread out over the countryside in little communities. Each group had a king and queen, with the queen having far the most power. Fairy women had several husbands apiece, which was one reason they were hated by the Christian church. The people revered and obeyed their rulers and one reason given for the decline of the race was the growing importance of the individual as opposed to authority.

Pride of fairy descent was so great that most kings of the north proudly claimed it. Various totem animals, bears, pigs, seals, can be seen on their shields today.

The clothing of fairy kings and queens was richer than that of their subjects. They often wore white silk or linen. In Kirkcudbrightshire, England, they wore crowns or pearl coronets and embroidered their garments with gold. Sometimes they wore a little red, as well as blue and green, but never yellow.

Men fairies in Ayershire looked and dressed like gentlemen, and women were "seemly-looking in plaids." The MacDonald banner in Scotland is known to have been made and given to the clan by fairies.

In Paleolithic times fairies lived in caves. Neolithic fairies built houses or huts. These huts, as described by Dr. Murray, continued as long as the fairies survived. They were circular, sunk two or three feet into the ground, and had stone floors. The walls were built of stone in the lower part, with turf or wattle-and-daub for the upper half. The turf roof, supported by a central post, had a smoke hole in the middle over the hearth which was in the center of the hut. Whole families lived together in these surprisingly roomy and comfortable homes.

Overgrown with grass, briars, and bushes, these huts looked like mounds or small hills, not houses. Their remains can be seen in open grassy country, writes Henry Treece, and sometimes still are called hut circles. They are marked on the official British Ordnance Survey maps. There is one of these circles of stone near Penzance in the heart of the "fairy country." A hundred years ago, when a railroad laid its tracks through a fairy mound near Belfast, Ireland, local residents predicted that the fairies would curse the road. A *Chicago Tribune* story of May 9, 1953, reports that the closure of the railroad, for reasons of economy, bore out this prophecy.

Because fairies were extremely shy and fleet of foot, they apparently were able to appear and disappear as if by magic. Their lives often depended on this ability.

Their food was mainly beef, milk, cream, butter, and cheese. They stole from village dairies, but were very generous also, pressing gifts of bread, butter, and cheese on those they visited. Most villagers left bread on their tables or hearths as gifts for the fairies in order to avoid trouble. They believed fairies could cast harmful spells on them, could poison them or their animals, steal their children, do all sorts of magic mischief. They were afraid of the Little People. Baking bread and cake was a noisy and gay fairy occupation. Often they could be heard outside their mounds by passersby. Made of corn flour, it was "the most delicious bread that ever I did eat, either before or since," J. Morgan, wrote in his *Phoenix Britannicus* in 1732.

One female friend of "a hee fayrie" had every night "for meat...capons, chickens, mutton, lambe, phesant, snite, woodcocke, partridge, quailes...wine she had of all sorts, muskadine, sacke, malmsie, clarret, white and bastard." They ate a great deal, loving banquets and feasts, which were served at clean covered tables. They had no metal pots, but would make rough, undecorated pottery. A silver chalice at Kirk Malew in the Isle of Man is said to have been stolen from the fairies.

Evidence that a villager dealt with fairies condemned him to be scourged, banished, or even burned at the stake. Despite this there was a good deal of intermingling, for they depended on villagers for some of the necessities of life, and even at times for the continuation of their race.

Because of their cleverness with medical herbs, fairy maidens sometimes hired out as housemaids, just as their brothers worked as herders, says Beauheimer. Their pictures on medieval manuscripts, love caskets, and tapestries show them as faithful housewives, camping out in the country. They often married townsmen, making faithful but not patient wives, for they were mistresses whose commands must be obeyed.

The fairies held joy ceremonies and dances on May Day, Midsummer Eve, and Halloween. Often they danced around fairy trees, such as the one at Domremy, France. Many of these trees became the groves of the Druids many centuries later, after the Aryans and the Celts. Our Maypole dance and the Furry Dance held annually at Helston, England, originated as fairy dances.

In spite of their gaiety they knew from necessity how to protect themselves. They could kill instantly with tiny arrows, a mere scratch from their arrow's hemlock poisoned barb was fatal. Their flint arrowheads were one inch long and half an inch wide, triangle-shaped with barbs on each side. These small elf-arrows are still found occasionally on open heaths and downs, says Treece, and may be seen in British museums. They were shot from small bows made of bog-weed, or flipped with the thumb like a marble.

Though they made flint arrows, axe-heads, and adzes, and delicate oval scraping-knives, they could not use iron. They feared and loathed it as a symbol of their defeat by the strong, bronze and iron-using Aryans. They hated church bells both for being iron and as the voice of the church which fought them.

Iron horseshoes were triple magic: they were connected with their favorite and sacred animal; they were bent in the shape of the crescent moon symbolizing one of the ancient goddesses; and they were made of iron, the hated metal. Our present superstition of "lucky" horseshoes is a leftover fairy belief, as is the idea that bad luck follows the gift of a knife or scissors to a friend, according to Pennethorne Hughes, in his book, *Witchcraft*.

As a racial group fairies are gone; but fairies were real and many remnants of their culture are with us still.

The Little Man in White

Eva Pashke
December 1957

When I was eight years old, we moved to a large house in Freeport, Illinois. That winter in 1906 was cold and my older stepsister, Dell, developed a bad case of pleurisy.

My stepmother was exhausted from trying to keep house and nurse Dell, so my father moved her to the bedroom downstairs, where it was warmer. He brought down two huge feather beds and put them on the floor. He told my sister Marcie, eleven years old, my stepsister, Ethel, thirteen years old, and me to sleep in the same room wi th Dell and to call him if there was any change in her condition.

The first thing we did after we were certain our parents were in the kitchen was to get into a pillow fight.

Suddenly Dell sat up in bed and started to sing "And Her, Name Was Rose" at the top of her voice. We stopped the pillow fight at once. Dell turned, still singing and evidently delirious, toward the door leading into the darkened living room. We turned, too.

Standing in the doorway was a little man about my height, stooped and leaning heavily on a gnarled cane. He was dressed in a tall, white hat, a white tuxedo-like suit, and a white cape. His face was wrinkled and angry-looking, his hair long, white, and slightly curled, his hands crippled with work or disease, his nails very long. He grimaced and showed ragged, fang-like teeth. Everything about him seemed to shimmer and glow.

Suddenly Ethel began screaming and Marcie and I joined in. The little man raised his cane, shook it, and started in our direction. We heard a shout from the kitchen and my father burst into the room. I was looking at the little man and he vanished instantly.

Dell fell back on the bed. She went into a deep sleep and in a few days was well again. Although my father inquired, no one in Freeport knew of any explanation for the little man and we never saw him again.

William Allen White and the Little People

UPI photo

Glenn Clairmonte
December 1972

The noted journalist William Allen White (1868–1944), who made Emporia famous and was one of the most prominent editors of his time, would seem an unlikely person to be accused of "seeing things." In politics he was the world's most skeptical and in judgment the world's most sober.

Yet in his *Autobiography* (Macmillan, 1946) he describes a vision he never was able to explain. Although he began the report by calling it "quite mad" he gave the details with his characteristic clarity.

In 1891 when he was still under 30 he was about to start what seemed a glamorous career as a Kansas City newspaper reporter. He spent his last evening at home in El Dorado, Kansas, saying farewell to all his lifelong friends. He then went to bed while the August harvest moon was still high in the sky and fell into a deep sleep. By the time the moon had traveled to where its beams were creeping through his window and across his face he awoke and decided it probably was two or three hours before sunrise.

He was about to turn his face away from the moonlight and go back to sleep when he heard the soft sound of rhythmic music. He leaned up on an elbow and looked out of the south window toward a huge elm tree, beneath which he only recently had mowed the blue grass.

To his immense surprise, he saw beneath that elm tree a variety of little people, three or four inches tall, gaily dancing together while humming with the music. Naturally he thought this was very unusual, to say the least, for there seemed no possible reason for such an occasion to be taking place in his family's yard. But the lucidity of the scene was too much for him to deny. He turned away and looked again. He did all he could to assure himself that he was mistaken. He even rose and walked across the room to look out another window but even from there he could see those dainty grayish little figures moving to the tune that flowed around them.

Again Bill White tried to prove to himself that he was awake and that he actually was seeing these little people whom he had never seen before at any time of day or night. He resolutely turned away and went back to bed but when he rose again they still were there. He executed some vigorous calisthenics to discharge any dreamlike mood but when he looked again he still could see those gentle activities beneath the elm tree.

Then as he watched them for at least five more minutes they began to fade, finally leaving only the blue grass for him to stare at.

In trying to analyze the situation he eventually decided that by some amazing quirk his optic nerves had caught some rays of reality that his eyes were not usually sensitive enough to catch. He reasoned there may be other creatures within our world "which we may not feel with our bodies attuned to rather insentient nerves." He told himself that "with other eyes other beings see other things; with other ears they hear much that escapes human ears."

Nevertheless he concluded the account by saying, "When I recall that hour I am so sure that I was awake I think maybe I am still crazy."

The Cottingley Fairies: A Hoax?

Robert Sheaffer
June 1978

The English village of Cottingley in Yorkshire is so small that it scarcely ever appears on a map. But an event which occurred there sixty years ago not only generated worldwide publicity but also precipitated a controversy that has not been fully settled today.

In 1917 two Cottingley girls produced what are said to be photographs of "fairies." While some persons accepted these as authentic, many others did not and greeted them with jeers and derision. No convincing evidence has ever been presented to show whether the photos are or are not authentic. Now, however, modern computer enhancement techniques may settle the question.

The process of photography was invented in the first half of the nineteenth century but not until 1920 were the first photographs of fairies published. They are said to have been taken in the summer of 1917 by Elsie

Wright, thirteen, and her cousin Frances Griffiths, ten, using Elsie's father's camera. The girls obtained three more fairy photos in 1920 and these were the last.

The five photographs show the girls in the company of an assortment of fairies and one gnome who dance on the banks of a stream, leap in the air, and offer a posy of harebells. The fairies not only have wings like a butterfly's but wear gossamer robes and play the panpipe—exactly like the classic fairies of folklore. Misidentification of the creatures is impossible—they are fairies. Thus, the photos are among the most significant and remarkable in human history—or they are a hoax.

The best-known proponent of the Cottingley fairy photos is the celebrated literary figure, Sir Arthur Conan Doyle, creator of Sherlock Holmes. Doyle was keenly interested in Spiritualism and many other esoteric subjects. It was Doyle who first brought the fairy photos to the public's attention in an article in the Christmas 1920 issue of *Strand* Magazine titled "The Fairies Photographed." The following year he expanded the article into a book, *The Coming of the Fairies,* which presents the most detailed discussion of the Cottingley incident ever written.

In many ways, however, the central figure in the controversy is not Doyle, but Edward L. Gardner, a member of the Executive Committee of the Theosophical Society in England. It was Gardner who brought the photos to Doyle's attention and performed an on-site investigation of the indicent. The case for the authenticity of the fairy photographs rests heavily on Gardner's work. (With good reason Doyle chose Gardner's portrait to appear on the frontispiece of his book.)

The Theosophical Society combines Eastern mysticism and Western occultism into a unique esoteric, metaphysical philosophy. One of many unusual doctrines supported by Theosophists is the belief that fairies do indeed exist, that they have evolved from creatures similar to butterflies, and that they perform for plants certain highly essential functions which are similar to photosynthesis.

At the time Doyle first became aware of the fairy photos (which he has hailed as "evidence for the actual existence of fairies") he had "by a curious coincidence" (his words) just completed an article titled "The Evidence for Fairies." It consisted of accounts of fairy sightings but offered no *tangible* proof for fairies' existence. Doyle was overjoyed when he heard through his Spiritualist friends that the Theosophical Society had in its possession what appeared to be the evidence he had been seeking. He began to make inquiries and finally obtained copies of the fairy photos from one Miss Blomfield, a cousin of E.L. Gardner.

Doyle soon got to know Gardner who said he had obtained the photos from a friend who had gotten them from Mrs. Wright, Elsie's mother, who for several years had been a follower of Theosophy. While some might think it was an odd coincidence that the supposed proof of the reality of fairies should come from the household of a Theosophist whose views support their existence, Conan Doyle saw no reason for suspicion.

According to the Wrights, both Elsie and her cousin Frances told of seeing fairies often and playing with them in the woods near their home. The parents say they dismissed this as mere childhood fantasy. Then one day in July 1917 Elsie persuaded her father to let them borrow his camera (which held just a single plate) so that they could attempt to photograph their fairy playmates. They reportedly went out alone and returned with a photograph showing several fairies dancing on the bank of a stream with Frances' face just behind them. Curiously, however, Frances is looking at the camera, not at the fairies. Gardner explains this by saying that while seeing fairies was an everyday occurrence for Frances, the camera was unusual!

Publication of the Cottingley photographs generated a storm of controversy, for few people outside of a small circle of Spiritualists, Theosophists, and other disciples of the occult took them seriously. Critics charged that the photos could easily have been faked in a photographer's studio—which is true. But Doyle and Gardner countered that just because the photos *could* be duplicated using trickery, it does not follow that trickery was used—

which is also true.

However, the "fairies" in the photographs look so flat, so patently false, that it is next to impossible for any thinking person to take them seriously. They look for all the world like a humorous fake, a parody of the quaint little creatures found in children's storybooks. Yet no specific flaws were ever detected either in the photographs or in the principals' stories to clearly indicate a hoax.

In recent years a number of books and articles have been published suggesting that whatever the UFO phenomenon may be, it is closely related to—if not the same as—the fairy sightings of old. A few UFO writers have even suggested that the Cottingley photographs, despite their faked look, may indeed be authentic. Having investigated a dumber of well-known, supposedly unexplained UFO photographs which turned out to be hoaxes, I decided to see if the photographic evidence for fairies might be more impressive.

It turned out that information on the fairy photographs was difficult to come by. Other than the books by Conan Doyle and Gardner and one by Theosophist G. L. Hodson, little additional information appeared to be available. The Theosophical Society in New York and the Theosophical Publishing House in Wheaton, Illinois, could not provide any new information. However, the Theosophical Society in London informed me that after E. L. Gardner's death, his son donated all of Gardner's material on the Cottingley incident, including the original photographs and documents, to the University of Leeds in Yorkshire. They are now part of the Brotherton Collection at the Brotherton Library and under the supervision of the Director of Folk Life Studies.

From the University of Leeds I obtained a list of the several hundred documents in Gardner's collection and purchased five-by-seven-inch copies of the five "fairy photographs." The prints are somewhat marred by dust on the copy negatives but they show a great deal more detail than the illustrations in Doyle's and Gardner's books. I mailed the set of five fairy photographs to William H. Spaulding, Western Division Director of Ground Saucer

Watch (GSW) in Phoenix, Arizona.

GSW uses computerized techniques for enhancing photographs of UFOs and few have been able to stand up to the analysis. Spaulding is the first to admit that his techniques are not infallible but in a significant number of cases, GSW's computer enhancement has turned up new information about the photos, causing them to be seen in a different light.

GSW's computer analysis breaks down a photograph into thousands of "pixels"—picture elements. The computer assigns a number to correspond to the brightness of a given point in the photo. By analyzing the relationships between these numbers across various regions of the photograph, the computer can bring out faint details not visible to the naked eye. Boundaries between objects are analyzed and whether or not an object is three-dimensional can be determined by the way light and shadow are distributed across its surface.

After running a full analysis on the fairy photographs, Spaulding reported: "...It is the conclusion of the entire GSW photographic staff that the images depicted herewith (the fairies) represent a hoax." He notes that all of the fairy images except one are flat, "probably made of cardboard." While the human faces in the photos are found to be obviously three-dimensional, the profile of the fairies shows absolutely no depth. Some flimsy cloth-like material appears to have been used to create the fairies' clothing. Their facial features appear to have been painted on, for brush marks are visible. The "gnome" in one of the photographs does appear to be three-dimensional. Spaulding speculates this may be a ceramic or porcelain statuette. The fairy offering a posy of harebells to Elsie appears to be supported by a thread which is visible in the enhanced photograph. On the basis of the shape of the "pixels," GSW analysts say the fairies are quite close to the camera and approximately six to eight inches in height.

Summing up, Spaulding concludes, "There is absolutely no photographic evidence to substantiate these 'fairy' photographs as authentic evidence. In essence these photographs represent a crude hoax."

How much confidence can we place in this conclusion? The "string" which appears to support one of the creatures is powerful evidence of a hoax. Unless a scratch can be shown to exist on the negative, precisely in the right position, we shall have to regard the apparent "string" as a real one and the photograph as a hoax. Also convincing is the computer's demonstration of the fairies' flat profile and the brush marks on their facial features. This, too, is difficult to refute—unless we hypothesize that fairies exist but are flat like wafers and wear gobs of thick makeup!

Even if all of GSW's evidence against the fairy photographs could be explained away, other strong evidence has been uncovered that suggests they are a hoax.

Elsie Wright and Frances Griffiths obtained a second series of fairy photographs in August 1920 under the guidance of E. L. Gardner. If the girls had already obtained two photographs of fairies, it seemed they should be able to take many more. Furthermore, critics would certainly challenge them to a repeat performance.

Hence Mr. Gardner supplied two cameras—one for each girl—and two dozen plates. No longer living together, the two girls said they could arrange to be together only for a single fortnight, because of school commitments and such. (Both of them had to be there, they explained, or they would be unable to produce any photographs.) Thus, during the second half of August 1920, Frances and Elsie took their cameras into the fairy glen.

One would expect that in the course of two full weeks the girls would have had little difficulty obtaining twenty-four clear and distinct photographs of fairies. After all, they claimed to see fairies nearly every time they went outside. *But only three photographs were obtained*—hardly an impressive number. Why didn't they obtain more? Because it rained almost the entire time, they said. They had been able to visit the fairy glen on only two afternoons. According to Gardner's book, *Fairies: The Cottingley Photographs and Their Sequel*, "During the second fortnight in August 1920 it rained almost continuously throughout the country. The papers reported the rain as general...."

Heavy rainfall would provide, of course, an explanation for why more fairy photos were not obtained—*if it had actually occurred.* However, according to *British Rainfall* for 1920, a journal published by authority of the British Meteorological Committee:

"August—Anticyclonic conditions prevailed during the middle and latter part of the month and the weather, though cool, was on the whole dry."

Bradford, the recording station nearest Cottingley, reports that the rainfall during August 1920 was only 62 percent of normal. Other weather stations in Yorkshire report as little as 31 percent of the normal rainfall. England as a whole averaged only 56 percent. Yet Gardner claims the newspapers were filled with stories of almost continuous rainfall at the time the girls were attempting, under his supervision, to obtain more fairy photographs!

These recent findings on the Cottingley incident make it impossible to take the fairy photographs at face value. I believe I have eliminated whatever slim grounds may have once existed for accepting their authenticity. And there are other reasons for doubt.

Now in their seventies, Elsie and Frances are still living and occasionally are asked about the photos. (They have appeared on BBC Television and an interview with them was published in the British magazine *Woman* for October 25, 1975.) Some of Elsie's remarks have been interpreted as confessing to the hoax. For example, she has said, "They're photographs of figments of our imagination."

Elsie is unable to say where the fairies came from when they appeared or where they went when they left. If her story is true, it would seem she must have seen them arriving and departing.

In the photos the girls are not looking directly at the fairies—which seems odd.

Finally, we must note how eagerly Gardner, having convinced Conan Doyle of the authenticity of the photos, launched upon an extended lecture tour with the now-famous photos, promoting his Theosophical doctrines.

Note: As Jerome Clark pointed out in "The Cottingley Fairies: The Last Word" in FATE, November 1978, the question of the authenticity of the Cottingley fairy photographs should have been settled once and for all by Fred Gettings in *Ghosts in Photographs* (Harmony Books, 1978). Gettings found three identical fairy drawings in *Princess Mary's Gift Book* (Hodder and Stoughton, 1915) done by the artist Claude A. Shepperson to illustrate "A Spell for a Fairy," a poem by Alfred Noyes.

Encounters with Little Men

Alex Evans
November 1978

It happened, the old man recalls, one morning early in May 1913. He was twelve years old and he and his brothers Sid and Clyde were chopping cotton on the family farm 2-1/2 miles west of Farmersville, Texas. There was no reason to believe this day would be unlike any other. Silbie Latham did not know then that he would remember it for the rest of his life.

The first hint that something out of the ordinary was about to occur was the sudden barking of the two dogs, Bob and Fox, who had been frolicking some distance away. It was not an ordinary bark, not the kind of sound they made when they had treed a possum or a polecat. It was, Latham says, "just like they was in a terrible distress."

The boys kept working but the "deathly howl" continued. Finally Clyde, the oldest, picked up his hoe and said, "Let's go up and see what them dogs treed. Must be somethin' pretty bad."

The three of them started walking toward the dogs, which were about

50 to 75 feet away on the other side of a picket fence.

Clyde got there first. When he looked down, the expression on his face turned to one of astonishment.

"It's a little man!" he shouted.

"I got there and I saw him," Latham remembers. "He looked like he was resting on something. He was looking toward the north. He was no more than eighteen inches high and kind of a dark green in color. He was the same smooth color all over.

"He didn't seem to have on any shoes but I don't really remember his feet. His arms were hanging down just beside him, like they was growed down the side of him. He had on a kind of hat that reminded me of a Mexican hat. It was a little round hat that looked like it was built onto him. He didn't have on any clothes. Everything looked like a rubber suit including the hat....

"He just stood still. I guess he was just scared to death...Right after we got there, the dogs jumped him."

The dogs tore the little man to pieces. Red blood spilled everywhere and the being's insides, which looked like human organs, fell to the ground. As the boys stood watching, the animals bit the man's legs off. If the being made any sounds as he was being killed, the Lathams could not hear them because of the racket the dogs were making.

"We were all just country as hell and didn't know what to do about it," Latham explains. "I guess we were just too dumb to think about it."

The boys returned to their hoeing and discussed the incident among themselves. Two or three times they went back to the spot to check the remains, which lay rotting in the sun. All the while the dogs huddled close by them as if frightened.

Later that day the boys told their parents, who didn't seem to take them seriously. The next day the three examined the spot where the being had lain but not a trace of it, not so much as a single bloodstain, remained. It had vanished completely. They searched the area for further evidence of what they had seen but found nothing.

Two years later, however, Silbie and one of his brothers saw something else out of the ordinary. While sitting on the porch of their uncle's farmhouse near Celeste, Texas, the Lathams watched a mysterious object carrying two lights—one in front, the other in back—sail silently by. In the early darkness they could make out a large cylindrical shape "like an airplane without wings" between the lights.

The report is reminiscent of others from the period. During the late nineteenth and early twentieth centuries numerous persons in Texas and other states said they saw unidentified "airships."

Three years after that the Latham brothers witnessed yet another odd event. At about eight o'clock one fall evening (Silbie Latham does not recall the exact year, only that it was before the end of World War I), Silbie and Sid saw a "ball of fire" about the size of a washtub fall out of the sky and hit the ground fifty feet behind their house. The two grabbed a lantern and rushed to the spot, where they found a light gray powder on the ground forming a rough circle about three feet in diameter. There was no indentation in the ground, as would have been the case if the falling object had been a meteorite.

The bizarre story of the little green man of Farmersville, Texas, remained unknown to the rest of the world until January 1978 when Silbie Latham's grandson Lawrence Jones, now of Austin, Texas, wrote the Center for UFO Studies about it. He said, "My grandfather has a most solid reputation for truth and honesty but has never told of this because of fear of ridicule.... He has agreed to tell this only after much prompting and encouragement from me, his history-oriented grandson. He would take a polygraph or be hypnotized or whatever you need. There is no question in my mind that he is telling the truth." Jones wrote that the subject "has been discussed in my family for many years."

Douwe Bosga, who was then investigative coordinator for the Center, asked Larry Sessions of the Fort Worth Museum of Science and History to look into the case. On April 28, 1978, Sessions interviewed Mr. Latham at length.

Sessions describes Latham as a "neat old man. I wouldn't mind having him for my own grandfather. A remarkable man."

But while he acknowledges Mr. Latham's obvious sincerity, Sessions still finds the story difficult to swallow. "There's no doubt he believes it happened," Sessions says, "but that doesn't mean it did happen. Maybe he has an overactive imagination. Or maybe his brothers played a trick on him and he's sort of unconsciously embellished the story over the years."

In his interview with Latham, Sessions even suggested that the little man was nothing more than a big frog—an idea the witness emphatically rejected.

Jones remains convinced that his grandfather saw what he says he saw.

Whatever the case, it appears that Mr. Latham is not the only person who believes he saw a little man during the second decade of the twentieth century. The late Harry Anderson saw twenty of them, according to his widow, Helen Anderson of Fort Atkinson, Wisconsin.

One hot summer's night in 1919 Anderson, then a thirteen-year-old boy, was driving with two friends and their father when their car ran out of oil and came to a stop east of Barron, Wisconsin. Not long afterward a local farmer who had been out fishing walked by. Told what had happened, he said he would give the stranded travelers some oil from his farm if one of them came along with him to the house.

Young Anderson agreed to go. Together he and the farmer walked the two miles to the farm. After getting the oil Harry started back along the one-track road.

The night was bright because of a full moon. So when Harry saw them, they were clearly visible.

"They" were twenty little men walking single file, heading toward him but paying no attention to him. Their heads were bald and the figures were dressed in leather "knee-pants," held up by suspenders over their shoulders.

They wore no shirts and their skins were white. They were "mumbling" but apparently not talking with one another.

Anderson, almost petrified with fear, continued on his way, not once looking back. When he got back to the car some time later, he told his friends what he had seen. They laughed at him.

After that he told only his mother, who didn't laugh—"after all," Mrs. Anderson explains with a chuckle, "she was Irish"—and, years later, his wife, who says, "My husband was not an imaginative person at all. He had no imagination whatsoever. This absolutely happened, as far as he was concerned. I mean there was no question about it."

The story has a peculiar sequel.

In 1969 or 1970 Mrs. Anderson wrote a short account of the incident and submitted it to FATE. She placed a carbon copy of the article in a drawer beneath her typewriter table. Several weeks later FATE's editors returned the manuscript.

She decided to put the original with the carbon copy. But when she opened the drawer, she discovered the copy was missing—although she knew with certainty that this was where she had been keeping it.

"Then about two weeks later I looked for the original and that was gone too," she says. "I certainly never got rid of them because I thought that someday I'd submit them to another magazine."

Neither has ever shown up.

"So I don't know," she says with a shrug and a small smile. "Maybe somebody's telling me not to say anything about it."

The Little Green Man Who Got Away

Robert Goerman
May 1982

On Sunday evening, March 1, 1981, I was watching *The Amityville Horror* on my twelve-inch black-and-white television screen when the telephone rang. I immediately recognized the voice as that of Arnold, Pennsylvania, Police Sgt. Jim Dargenzio, an old friend.

"Bob, where were you last night?" he asked. "I tried to reach you on this situation we got here. Seems some boys encountered some really weird creature by the railroad tracks...less than three feet tall, all green, wrinkled skin, long arms. . . .

"The rub is that one of the boys picked the damned thing up and tried to carry it home! The thing wriggled free. Didn't hurt him or anything. It fled into a drainpipe and got away. But it's been seen since. Seems to be sticking around."

After Jim filled me in, Police Chief Bill Clark telephoned and added his ten cents' worth. It was clear the officers were taking the bizarre story seriously and requesting my unofficial assistance. The Arnold police department wanted me to catch the thing.

Living in the city, where a backyard to an apartment dweller is often no more than a window box three stories up, kids are naturally attracted to those areas where there is room to stretch. In Arnold one such area is Roosevelt Park, a block-long playground complete with amphitheater and war memorials as well as an auxiliary policeman who oversees safety.

But safety never was a teen watchword. Kids crave adventure, especially when there's the slightest hint of danger associated with it.

Small wonder then that four brothers—Bobby Johnston, sixteen; Marvin, thirteen; David, twelve; and Chris, eleven—and their friend Randy Uhler, twelve, sought out the Penn Central switchyard, with its even rows of boxcars and tankers, bunkers and trees, and the like, just as they did every other Saturday afternoon. Here was a battlefield strewn with enemy tanks, a fortress to be assaulted by commando forces, a Martian landscape, and more.

As they were playing, young Chris saw what he thought was a green trash bag. Curious, he approached it. Now it looked more like a statue, a big green statue. Of a man? But what kind of man?

The statue moved.

Not much. But it moved.

The thing was squatting down along the railroad track beside a gray tank car loaded with salts. Its back was to Chris, who was a mere fifty feet away.

"I just had to take it home," Chris would tell me, "or nobody would believe me!"

His mother added, "That boy is always bringing something home and hiding it in our basement—anything he can get his two little mitts on and carry home."

Chris ("Bring 'Em Back Alive") Johnston edged forward, carefully stepping only on the railroad ties, avoiding the crackling cinders and gravel. He could not call for help now. The thing might run.

His arms snaked under the thing's armpits, lifted up and locked his fingers against the back of its neck—the standard wrestler's full-nelson grip.

Now Chris screamed for help. "Bobby! Marvin! Help me carry this home!" he shouted. His brothers and friend rushed to his aid.

Bobby, Marvin, and company froze in their tracks. They could handle turtles, even snakes, but this was something else. Later, when interviewed separately, the boys agreed that the "something" was green in color with no hair or fur. Humanoid in shape, it had wrinkled "elephant" skin, stood just under three feet tall and walked upright on two legs. It also had a muscular chest with distinct nipples, a tiny one-inch tail, and large ears. Chris told me that the skin felt dry and rubbery, stretched like elastic.

"Bobby! Help! It's too strong!" Chris shrieked.

It wriggled and twisted and squealed and wriggled. Older brother Bobby, five years the wiser, offered this advice: "Drop it and get out of there!" That sentiment having been expressed, Bobby took to his heels.

If the others thought to help Chris, it was too late. The thing broke free of the boy's grasp and shot into a drainpipe less than eight feet away.

"Those boys were really excited and upset when we arrived on the scene," Sergeant Dargenzio said. "We were checking a robbery in the area when we saw them running. They thought we were the reinforcements, so to speak, that someone had called us to help them capture this green thing."

Mrs. Johnston told police her son's coat had a foul odor "like a dirty fish tank" where it came into contact with the creature.

The next morning I met with Chief Clark and received a copy of Chris' sketch of the thing made under rather harried conditions in the back of a patrol car. The Arnold police are hard-nosed, cynical cops who have seen and heard every tale in the book: They are anything but gullible; yet they were convinced that the boys had seen something far out of the ordinary. At 11:45 a.m. I drove to the scene and checked it out. Before I left, I inspected the drainpipe. Lying there on my stomach while I stuck head and lantern into the pipe, I halfway expected to come eyeball-to-eyeball with the twilight zone's answer to Kermit the Frog. But the pipe was empty. In addition, the ground was rocky, eliminating any possibility of tracks.

Before leaving the site, I deployed bait, six apples cut into quarters, in what I deemed strategic locations. A fine sprinkling of powder (to enhance tracks) added a final touch.

Late that afternoon I returned to find the site surrounded by teenagers. Rain had washed away the powder and several slices of apple had disappeared. I noticed that one piece had been chewed on. I fished it out for examination and noted clear, well-defined teeth marks—those of a rat.

Minutes later, upon my arrival at Arnold police headquarters, I saw a scowling desk officer inform a caller that an investigation into reports of a "green thing" was under way. He put down the phone long enough to tell me that calls were flooding in.

By seven o'clock that evening dozens of teenagers were prowling the site. Many were armed with rocks, pellet guns, clubs, and flashlights. Cars slowed down and paused on the road above, their occupants jeering. So much for my low-key investigation.

The next day pandemonium ruled. The local newspaper, *Valley News Dispatch,* was working on a "green monster" piece. I met the reporter, Mike Burke, and urged him not to ridicule the witnesses and to emphasize that this thing was apparently not aggressive or harmful.

I also talked with Marvin Johnston over the phone. In the afternoon I came back to the site, which was overrun with kids.

Knowing that serious investigation was impossible under these circumstances, I returned home until 9:00 p.m. Then I drove back and began to patrol a mile-long stretch of railroad tracks. It was a miserable experience. The rain was turning to snow and the temperature was dropping. Seven hours later, at 4:00 a.m. I finally got to bed.

Late the following morning, March 4, I was back patrolling the tracks. This time I found something: seven branches, about one inch thick and seven inches long, broken off evenly with bark chewed off like corn-on-the-cob. This was nothing deer would have done, but as evidence of anything it wasn't much.

But if hard evidence was difficult to come by, wild rumors were all too abundant. The creature was credited with attacking and raping an eight-year-old girl, chewing the leg off a policeman, overturning a New Kensington patrol car. and so on and on into the wild blue yonder. The head of the Arnold PTA called the police to ask if these stories were true. Police department switchboards were flooded again.

At 9:00 a.m. on March 5 I talked with reporter Burke at the *Dispatch.* He told me his first story draft had been rejected because his editors feared it would further "incite public hysteria." The word came down to keep it light and humorous. I had to agree.

I later interviewed Sandy Uhler, the attractive and articulate mother of 12-year-old Randy, one of the original witnesses. "My son isn't lying," she declared emphatically. "He and the other kids were all genuinely frightened and upset by this experience. I'd rather not believe his story because I don't like the idea of that creature lurking about. I hope you catch it—to end this ridicule."

Halfway through my interview Chris Johnston walked into the Uhler home on his school lunch break. I showed him a sketch of the creature I had drawn. He confirmed its accuracy.

From there I journeyed to the Arnold police station, where I was handed the logbook. At 7:40 the previous evening, it reported, two police officers had searched the 1600 block of Horne Boulevard for a "three-foot lizard."

I talked with the patrolman who interviewed the witness, a Glen C. (name withheld by request), a man in his 40s and the first adult witness.

At 3:00 P.M. the *Valley News Dispatch* hit the stands complete with a front-page story, headlined "Green Thing Sparks Rumors," that made light of the scare. Reading it, I reflected that not only would no witness in his right mind *ever* report a sighting after this, but previous witnesses would probably begin reneging their testimony!

By the next day a fresh rumor was circulating. This one claimed that the creature had been captured by the police who delivered it to the Pittsburgh Zoo. It was an iguana.

In reality, of course, iguanas, like other reptiles, are cold-blooded animals. Any reptile subjected to that week's cold weather (between the high twenties and low thirties) would have become sluggish in very short order, then turned immobile before entering a state of deep hibernation. In any case all local police departments denied the iguana story.

Shortly after six o'clock I was back at the site when suddenly a "Green Monster" approached me and asked, "What's up, Doc?" while chewing on a candy bar. It was a kid, about nine or ten, wearing tennis shoes and a T-shirt emblazoned with a green thing with a drooping tongue. The words provided positive identification: "Green Monster, Arnold, Pennsylvania." He told me he had just bought the shirt at a local department store where they were selling like hotcakes.

Four hours later, on a final visit, I found a crowd of excited men bent forward and staring at something on the ground: a six-inch print with three toes. The men began pouring the plaster for the cast. I hadn't the heart to tell them that it looked very much as if a dog had slid in the mud and erosion had mutilated the print.

"It was a dinosaur-type thing, but yet—" Sherry Coover paused as she sought the right words. "It was human, a child. Definitely not an animal."

I was impressed. I had done nothing to lead my star witness. I had not placed words or impressions into her mind. But her remark that it was "human, not an animal," substantiated what the other witnesses had said.

"It must really fear people, the way it took off so quickly when we approached it," the twenty-three-year-old brunette said when we talked on Monday, May 11, nine weeks after her sighting. "I won't give you their names but I saw some kids douse it with gasoline and set it aflame. Disgusting! Good thing most of the gas went everywhere but on this creature. So it wasn't really hurt."

Sherry Coover, her brother Mike, eighteen, daughter Sandy, four, and acquaintance Robert Stoner, seventeen, had their encounter on that fateful Sunday, March 1, at approximately 11:00 p.m. Until now they had told no one but close friends and family.

It was fortunate that Sherry and I have a mutual friend: Joe Spano, owner of Spano's Tropical Breeze, Arnold's finest and only pet store. Spano steered me to this all-important, multiple-witness episode.

"My daughter saw it first—and screamed," Sandy related. "It was standing upright in one of those large garbage-dumpster thingamajigs—you know, those square jobs with twin lids. It was picking up food, I guess.

"We all got a good look at it before it jumped out of the dumpster and took off on all fours. Could it ever move fast! We followed it as fast as we could. The whole area is lit up pretty good to cut down on the crime rate. It disappeared down this drainpipe."

The "dumpster" was located right along Fifth Ave., right in the heart of town, alongside a housing project—and, yes, right along a single railroad line, a spur leading from the industrial district bordering the Allegheny River to a convenient railroad switching area frequented by bored adolescents nearly every Saturday.

Behold the Kingdom of the Nature Gods

Rosemary Ellen Guiley
May and June 1994

I once lived in a house tucked into the woods in southern Connecticut. I felt as though I'd acquired my own private nature preserve. I could sit on the back deck and look out over a brook populated with muskrats and ducks, trees filled with an abundance of birds—and, everywhere, nature spirits. I was acutely aware of their presence, sensing them with my inner eye: silvery and white beings that zipped and flitted about the woods. I could only hold them in my consciousness for a moment at a time. I was especially fond of gazing out the big picture window at night—and particularly on nights when moonlight glittered through the trees—feeling the place alive with magic.

My awareness of the nature spirits was part of my own unfolding awareness of other realms of beings, especially the angelic kingdom. I have plenty of company. Even a cursory glance at the media, New Age literature, and programs for alternative learning centers shows a great upwelling of interest in communing with other realms. We are having encounters with the beings in these realms. We want to know what's going on. Besides angels, nature spirits called devas are talking to us. How do we answer back?

They have an agenda, and this is it: to be whole, we must have a sense of oneness and community with all creation. The nature spirits, following God's will, have made themselves available to open the lines of communication with humans—lines that have grown weak from disuse—and to help foster spiritual growth.

What is a Deva?

Many people refer to nature spirits as "devas." In Sanskrit, "deva" means "shining one." The term conjures up an image of an angel-like being who manifests in brilliant light. However, there is no single definition of a deva, nor is there any unilateral agreement as to what a deva is and does.

In popular Western occultism, a deva is an advanced spirit or god- being, who governs the elementals and the well-being of all things in nature.

In Hinduism, the term "deva" has various meanings. It is a brahman in the form of a personal God. A brahman is an abstract concept expressing absolute being or absolute consciousness, a state of pure transcendence that defies precise description. A deva also is a mortal who has attained a state of divinity, but remains mortal. And, a deva is also an enlightened person who has realized God.

In Buddhism, a deva is a god who lives in one of the good celestial realms (there are twenty-eight altogether). Such devas enjoy a long and happy life in these realms as rewards for good lives while mortals. However, they are subject to the wheel of reincarnation. Their very happiness in their realm is an obstacle to their enlightenment, for they cannot come to terms with the truth of suffering, one of the four noble truths that form the basis of Buddhist philosophy. The truth of suffering holds that everything is suffering: birth, illness, death, dislikes, desires, and attachments of the personality.

The concept of devas was introduced to the West largely through the writings of Helena P. Blavatsky, co-founder of the Theosophical Society in the late nineteenth century. According to Blavatsky, devas are types of angels or gods who can neither be propitiated nor worshipped by men. She quoted an Ascended Master, one of her mentors, as describing the devas, also called "Dhyan-Chohans," as progressed entities from a previous planetary period. In the evolution of new solar systems, the devas arrive before either elementals or man, and remain dormant until a certain stage of human evolution is reached. At that time, the devas become an active force and integrate with the elementals to further the development of man. In classical Greece, Blavatsky said, a class of devas became symbolized by Prometheus, symbol of the purely spiritual man.

Thus through Theosophy, the philosophy expounded by Blavatsky, devas came to be regarded as high-level nature spirits. Modern views vary as to whether devas are part of, or work under, the angel kingdom. Channeled messages from devas have increased during the latter twentieth century as part of the New Age movement. Such messages have tended to focus on the devas' displeasure with humans' pollution of the earth and disrespect for nature, but are tempered with the devas' offer of love to help us get our spiritual act together.

Descriptions and impressions about devas are, like angels, subjective and dependent upon the experiencer. Some individuals perceive detailed hierarchies of beings, while others say that devas, angels and nature beings are facets of a whole—like a diamond—and resist categorization. What one person calls a deva, another calls an angel.

"Both words can mean the same thing," said Sylvia Schechter, co- founder, with her husband, Lawrence, of the Alcyone Light Centre in Hornbrook, California, a Findhorn-like community where activities are done in consultation with devas and angels. "All created life is energy. The angel presences are huge accumulations of light energy. that lights, like archetypes, is so vast and tremendous that the human eye cannot behold it—they must step it down for us."

Devas themselves may remain invisible to the percipient, or manifest as human-like bodies of light, balls or points of light, or diffuse fields or grids of energy. They communicate via mental impressions, intuitions, the inner voice, or sometimes a clairaudient external voice, much like the daimon who whispered in Socrates's ear. The daimon, according to the Greeks, was an intermediary spirit between humanity and the gods, and could be either good or evil in intent. Socrates claimed his daimon was of good intent, and could be relied upon to sound warnings whenever he was in danger or in bad company. The daimon, he said, was even more trustworthy than the most reliable oracles of the times, the flights and entrails of birds.

In modern occultism, devas are most associated with nature, Mother Earth and planetary consciousness, and agriculture. Gardeners who work devas consider them to be "architects" of nature; one is assigned to every living thing, even the soil. Devas design blueprints for all living things, and orchestrate the energies necessary for growth and health. Devas dispense advice on planting, fertilizing, watering and general plant care, as well as how to eliminate pests such as moles and worms without killing them. The relationship with devas goes much deeper, to include a heightened respect for all living things and for nature, to work with unseen realms in love and cooperation, and to realize the interconnectedness of all things and to God.

The Findhorn Magic

Blavatsky may have set the stage for popular conceptions of devas as nature spirits, but the biggest boost in that direction came from Findhorn, an unusual community in northern Scotland—not far from the Arctic Circle—that became renowned in the late 1960s and the 1970s for spectacular produce grown with the advice of devas.

Findhorn describes itself as an "international spiritual community," with about 150 residents, plus supporters. It was founded on the principles that "God, or the source of life, is accessible to each of us at all times, and that

Cullerne Garden at Findhorn.

nature, including the planet, has intelligence and is part of a much larger plan. While we have no formal doctrine or creed, we believe an evolutionary expansion of consciousness is taking place in the world, creating a human culture infused with spiritual values." Findhorn is a charitable trust foundation, and offers various spiritual educational and training programs.

The founders of Findhorn were Peter and Eileen Caddy, husband and wife, and their friend, Dorothy Maclean. In 1962, the three found themselves out of work in Scotland—they had for years worked together running resort hotels—and had no recourse but to band together at the Findhorn Bay Caravan Travel Park, where the Caddys, with their three children, had their trailer. The trailer park was a desolate place to live—situated next to a rubbish dump and a rundown building—but Peter Caddy felt he had been directed there for a purpose through spiritual guidance that Eileen had received in meditation.

The Caddys had, in fact, primed their spiritual pump for years with study and practice, and, in Peter's case, by studying Rosicrucianism. Peter had tried to cultivate the psychic gifts that would enable him to have visions and receive messages, but such dramatic manifestations did not develop for him. He did, however, develop a keen sense of intuition—which is one important means of communing with the spirit world. Eileen Caddy, on the other hand, was able to develop mediumistic gifts, and produced daily writings from her meditations with God.

Maclean, too, had developed her own gifts, and had for years channeled divinely inspired messages. Around 1950–1951, she came into awareness of the God within. The experience transformed her life. She had become acquainted with the Caddys while they were all under the same spiritual tutor, a Quaker woman named Sheena Govan. (Govan's parents had founded an evangelical movement, the Faith Mission. Govan and Peter were married for five years.) Maclean also had become steeped in Sufism through her ex-husband.

Unable to find work, Peter Caddy turned to gardening to pass the time, even though Findhorn seemed the worst place imaginable to grow anything. Located on a narrow sandy peninsula jutting into the North Sea, it is exposed to near-constant winds from all sides, and its soil is ill-suited for gardening.

The first sign that they were engaged in a unique undertaking came in May 1963. One day during her daily meditation, Maclean received an unusual message about the "forces of Nature," and that one of her jobs was to attune and harmonize with those forces, who would be friendly in their greeting to her. Peter interpreted it to mean that she could get guidance from Nature on what to do in the garden. This was immediately affirmed in her next meditation, with a message that cooperation not only would be possible, but would be welcomed with great joy. The communicating being told Maclean that she could attune to nature spirits and the higher nature spirits over them, that is, the spirits of the clouds, rain, and vegetables. As Maclean describes in her autobiography, *To Hear the Angels Sing* (1980; 1990), she was told, "In the new world to come these realms will be open to humans—or should I say, humans will be open to them. Just be open and seek into the glorious realms of Nature with sympathy and understanding, knowing that these beings are of the Light, willing to help but suspicious of humans and on the lookout for the false. Keep with me and they will not find it, and you will all build towards the new."

Maclean did as instructed, and so began a long and fruitful relationship with the angelic and devic kingdoms. The first nature spirit to come into her awareness was the "Pea Deva," which she described as holding the archetypal pattern in place for all the peas in the world. Her primary contact emerged as the "Landscape Angel," who acted as control and had a broad, holistic outlook. The Landscape Angel often facilitated communication between Maclean and other beings. All communications were on the inner planes.

Initially, Maclean did not know what to call the beings with whom she came in contact. She thought them to be angels, but the term "angel" conjured up to her hackneyed religious and pop culture images. These beings seemed too glorious. She settled on the term "deva," though in talking about them, she used the terms "angel," "deva," and "nature spirit" interchangeably. She never saw these beings with external vision, but sensed them on the inner planes. They were of awesome scope, she said. Their duties were to hold the archetypal pattern of all material things in place—even man-made objects such as machines—and to offer love to humankind.

Within a year, under the guidance of the devas, Findhorn had been transformed. The gardens were, in Peter's terms, "overflowing" with life. Cabbages, which normally reach four pounds at maturity, weighed over forty pounds. Broccoli grew so large they were too heavy to lift from the ground.

In 1966, a friend of Peter Caddy's, scholar R. Ogilvie Crombie, paid a visit to Findhorn, an experience that opened him psychically. Shortly afterward, Crombie was sitting in the Royal Botanic Gardens near his home in Edinburgh, Scotland, when he saw a nature spirit dancing in front of him. The three-foot high, half-man, half-animal gave his name as Kurmos, and said he lived in the gardens and helped trees to grow. This meeting paved the way for a subsequent meeting with Pan, chief of the nature spirits. Pan told Crombie that he had been chosen to help renew the lost contact between mankind and the nature spirits. Crombie passed on to Caddy and the others at Findhorn what he learned from Pan about the spirits who lived and worked in the garden.

Meanwhile, the Caddys and Maclean were reluctant to talk about their invisible helpers, though word of their spectacular gardening successes spread. Agronomists could not explain their results, based just on the composition of the soil, and the methods they used. When they finally began to talk of the devas, they attracted disciples who wanted to live and work with them.

Findhorn became a model community for proponents of the New Age movement. It grew by leaps and bounds, and attracted many Americans. By the early 1970s, it boasted nearly 300 people, among them American philosopher David Spangler. Residents viewed themselves as the vanguard of a new society based on the principles of cooperation between man and the kingdom of nature.

Brian Nobbs, a British professional potter and artist, arrived at Findhorn in 1970, to find the place filled with magic and light. Nobbs, who ran the pottery, became Crombie's heir apparent with the community of Pan. It proved to be a purposeful passing of the spiritual wand, for Crombie died in 1974, and Nobbs has been instrumental in the preservation of the devic presence at Findhorn.

In the summer of 1971, Nobbs traveled to Edinburgh, and was invited by Crombie to spend the weekend with him. Crombie suggested that they spend a day visiting various places of devic importance, including the Royal Botanic Gardens. Crombie instructed Nobbs to be as aware as possible. "When you notice something, tell me," he said. "But I won't give you any clues."

The day was momentous, in which Nobbs experienced a tremendous expansion of consciousness that was, he said, "mind-shattering." One of the

A greenhouse at Findhorn.

most potent sites was the Royal Botanic Gardens, where Crombie himself had first encountered Pan.

"It was as though the scales dropped away from my eyes and senses," said Nobbs. "Everything was magnified dozens of times. I found myself wading through waves of energy rippling around my ankles like electrical currents." Crombie explained to him that these were energy lines connecting different points, like leys. Nobbs's attention then was directed off to one side of their path, where he sensed, with his inner vision, a being standing and regarding them. It was Pan. "Yes," agreed Crombie, when Nobbs told him of his impression. "Pan has been wondering how long it would take you to notice him."

At the Hermitage, Nobbs walked about feeling a beam of light that entered him through the top of his head. He became aware of beautiful, human-like beings about four feet in height who accompanied them. "I wasn't seeing this with my physical eyes," he said. "I thought I was mad." But the impressions were real. Crombie called the beings "high elves" after J. R. R. Tolkien's popular *Lord of the Rings* fantasy novels. The beings seemed happy to be described that way.

Ogilvie then explained that the purpose of this encounter was for one of the beings to accompany him back to Findhorn, in order to make a link with the garden and the power points in it. "And travel with me he did," said Nobbs. "I took the bus back to Findhorn, and he sat in the seat beside me. It was a very strange experience."

In late 1972, Nobbs departed Findhorn to spend three years in a Benedictine monastery. His intention was to devote the rest of his life to contemplative inner work, but it was not his vocation. It did serve to put his spiritual experiences into a perspective. He returned to Findhorn in 1979 for a year. The place had undergone dramatic change. It was much smaller, which was good, but it was burdened by debt, and key people like Maclean and Spangler had left. Nobbs was disappointed to observe that the magic and wonder at communion with the nature kingdom had been observed by a more rationalistic viewpoint. Without a focal point like Maclean, the connection to the devas had receded to a back burner. "I realized that it wasn't a permanent situation," Nobbs said. "I was guided to be patient."

In 1980, Peter and Eileen Caddy parted company, and Peter went to America (Eileen remains at Findhorn, but has taken a background role so that others can learn how to guide the community). Nobbs also left Findhorn in 1980, going to Pennsylvania to live and work for seven years. In Poconos Summit, he encountered Pan again in another, native guise.

Nobbs lived in an area where there were few houses, and the garden abutted a forest. The nights were heavy with magic. "One night I woke up to see the room flooded with a bright green light," Nobbs said. "I found I couldn't move—I was paralyzed. standing by the bed was an Indian in a loin cloth and a beaded necklace. He was green and his head touched the ceiling, which meant he was about nine feet in height." The being simply regarded Nobbs—no message was transmitted. Nobbs was not frightened, despite his inability to move. After a short time, the figure faded away.

Nobbs was puzzled about the identity of the Indian. Several years later, he read in a book about the Indian deity, "Living Solid Face" or "The Mask Being," who ruled over the forests and wild things. It was another aspect of Pan.

Nobbs encountered this entity again, two years ago, while in Florida near St. Petersburg. He was walking along an urban street, thinking about Pan, and suddenly felt the weight of an invisible arm around his shoulder. It was his old friend, Pan. The two communed silently for about a hundred yards, and then Pan departed. The purpose of the encounter seemed to be to let Nobbs know that the beings of the nature kingdom are with us always, even in urban environments.

Nobbs returned to work at Findhorn in 1990, where he has since run the pottery. He is an associate member of the Findhorn community, but lives nearby in the city of Elgin. Since his return, he has seen the link to the nature kingdom grow and strengthen. He is among those facilitating the renewal, and gives workshops on attuning to the devic world.

Such attunement, he said, is available to anyone who seeks the path of wholeness, and fosters awareness of all kingdoms. "There is a new consciousness emerging," said Nobbs. "I've seen an exponential increase in the sense of attunement. There are people being born with knowledge of the past and a readiness for this—hardly anything needs to be done to make it complete."

Indeed, Findhorn, more than any other community, event, or organization, has opened the gates to communication with the angelic and devic realms. When Maclean and the Caddys first began to publicize their devic helpers, they were surprised at the public response. Numerous other persons around the world said they, too, had established contact with the devic realm, but had remained quiet about it out of fears of ridicule.

Now, two decades or so later, rapport with devas has become accepted in certain circles, and increasing numbers of persons are seeking the attunement. Findhorn has served as the model for other similar gardens and communities around the world.

Planetary Citizen

Since leaving Findhorn, Dorothy Maclean has continued her rapport with the devic/angelic world. For the last eight or nine years, she has lived in Issaquah, Washington, not far from Seattle, where she stays in close touch with Spangler and other friends from Findhorn, who call themselves "The Lorian Association." She lectures and gives workshops.

Maclean now considers "angels" a more appropriate term than "devas" for what she experiences, but agrees that labels can be problematic, and humans must get beyond labels. She stills perceives these beings with the inner eye, and sees them as energy fields or force fields. Communion occurs when she can become one with their energy. "I get into my own soul level," she explained. "I can't do it if I'm upset or angry. You have to reach them through love and gratitude. We need their love, but they need ours, too."

After Maclean returned to North America, a new dimension of the angelic world opened to her when she began attuning to angels of cities. A country woman at heart, Maclean had never been fond of living in cities. But city angels changed her attitude. Relative to nature spirits, the city angels—all those angels who work with groups of humans—have a difficult job. "Cities are where the worst of humans comes out in terror and fear," she said. "But I realized that God is there, too. The angels are asking for our love to help them do their job."

Maclean then spent eight years living in downtown Toronto—without problem. "I had always believed that I was a planetary citizen," said Maclean, "but when I went to Toronto, I appreciated my Canadian nationality." She tuned into the Angel of Canada, and experienced a pure nature energy, but also a sense that Canada hadn't yet found its identity.

Maclean also tuned into the Angel of America, and sensed an identity of "freedom at all costs." Both Canada and the United States are experiments in freedom in government, the angels told her. Canada is more restrained than the U.S., but has less violence. The United States' destiny is at some point to join Canada.

In her travels, Maclean often tunes into the angels of countries and cities. It helps her quickly establish a rapport with her environment, and with the people she meets. She cautions, however, not to place undue emphasis on angelic rapport. "Attuning to the God within is most important," Maclean said.

Green Hope Farm

For Molly Sheehan, founder of Green Hope Farm in Meriden, New Hampshire, the psychic opening that led to communion with the devic and angelic kingdoms began with family tragedy.

In 1984, her second child, Elizabeth, was born with a cleft palate. As is common with this condition, little Elizabeth was deaf, and would remain so until her palate could be repaired. It was a stressful situation with which Sheehan found herself unable to cope well. She and her husband, Jim, relied totally upon the advice of doctors—advice which, she says, put Elizabeth in jeopardy. Sheehan became unable to nurse her baby. Her intuition told her how to remedy the problem—a bottle with a hose for feeding—but it meant going against medical advice.

With the well-being of her child at stake, Sheehan realized she had to follow her intuition. "We'd turned everything over to the doctors," she said. "I realized I had to take back my power." Other women find themselves in similar positions, she said. On a gut level, they know what they need to do, know their own power—but they don't always act on it out of fear, lack of confidence, or arguments from others.

Elizabeth recovered, and the Sheehans found new medical help. Elizabeth had two operations. At age nine months, her palate was repaired and she acquired her hearing.

But the stress for Sheehan was by no means over. She pondered why the birth defect had to happen in the first place. She found little solace from her conventional religious background. "I had always been active in church, but didn't pursue any truth," she said. "Now I had to take the paper bag off my head. I thought, 'What do I have to lose? I can't be in any more pain than I am.'

The pain opened doors to new spiritual corridors. Books literally fell off shelves—just like actress Shirley Maclaine experienced when she began her own spiritual quest. Teachers appeared. Sheehan discovered the Ascended Masters. Life took on a new dimension. In a nutshell, Sheehan learned to believe in herself, detach, and trust in God.

"I'm very grateful for what happened to Elizabeth," said Sheehan, finding the positive in an otherwise trying situation. "It absolutely cracked open my life. I had to throw out everything I had believed up until then. I learned that everything is purposeful and for learning, not necessarily for punishment."

The story with Elizabeth has a happy turn. A bright child of ten now, she enjoys the gift of clairvoyance, and sees the angels and devas at Green Hope Farm with her external vision. There are two other children in the Sheehan family—Ben, twelve, and Emily, five. They're all "old soul" children, said Sheehan. "They know they're God."

Green Hope Farm as a devic-human cooperative enterprise got its genesis while Sheehan was going through her spiritual questing. She was raised a farm girl in rural northeastern Connecticut, and she and Jim had moved to Meriden fifteen years ago. She'd always loved to garden, and almost considered it a "tremendous vice" that got in the way of other pursuits.

One day something shifted in her consciousness. "I started getting little messages," Sheehan said. "The asparagus would say something to me. I started to listen."

What she tuned into were the voices of angels, devas, and elementals, who began to give her gardening guidance. They told her what, how, and when to plant, how to cultivate, and also how to design gardens.

Sheehan, who does not see these beings but hears them via an inner voice, prefers not to precisely define them. "They say they are a spectrum of energy," she said. "It is humans who have put the labels 'angel' and 'deva' on them.

They don't deal in a world of language, and won't resolve the issue of labels for me—they don't think that's important. They would rather have me recognize them by their different vibrations."

In terms of their vibrations, Sheehan senses that devas generally have a "bigger" energy than do angels, and are more evolved. But the picture is not clear-cut, for the energy of the archangel Michael, for example, is bigger yet. Again, Sheehan stressed that definitions simply don't work in this realm. She has been taught not to work in language, but in intuition and an inner "knowingness."

Initially, Sheehan would spend hours in meditation to in order to communicate with her unseen partners. Over the years, she has perfected her ability so that communication is much easier. Generally, she spends mornings writing down messages, but her spirit partners are always with her.

The purpose of Green Hope Farm, said Sheehan, is to demonstrate how the angelic, elemental, and human kingdoms can work harmoniously together and with God. The angelic kingdom holds the vision and divine plan for the place, and inspires the human kingdom with love and inspiration. The elementals bring the divine plan into physical form, using humans as their "hands and feet." The elementals are now bringing fifth-dimension energies into manifestation at Green Hope, as part of the expansion of consciousness underway for humanity.

There are three principal angels who work closely with Sheehan and others engaged in the work at Green Hope. Thela, Sheehan's primary contact for years, has been joined by Raphael, who holds the energy of love at the land, and Immanuel, who holds the energy of wisdom.

During the first five years of Green Hope Farm's existence, Sheehan was the only primary person involved. She learned, she said, to let go of her ego needs and "let God." In 1993, the angels told her to open the farm to more people, and three others joined in: Anita Walling, Susan Sanzone, and Shifra Levine. They call themselves the Four Winds Partnership. As a group, they had to learn to let go of their collective ego needs.

Green Hope Farm has ten gardens, all of which were planned in meetings with Thela, Pan, the God within, and the Ascended Masters. This group decides on the geometric configuration of each garden, as well as what will be planted and how it will be tended and harvested. The invisibles experiment and modify sometimes as work goes along. The shape of the garden is crucial, for it determines the energies that will manifest. Shapes changes every season.

Each garden radiates a different healing energy—they are, said Sheehan, grounding new energies on the planet. People report that they can feel this energy just from walking through the gardens, or meditating in them. The land radiates powerful energies even when fallow, she said.

Gardens are devoted to aromatic plants, herbs, perennials, vegetables, and a nature sanctuary that is set aside exclusively for the elementals to enjoy. The main vegetable garden for the 1994 season is in the shape of a Star of David, with vegetable in the colors of the Seven Rays.

In addition, there is Elizabeth's Garden; an "S Bed," which will bear new species arriving from other worlds; a flower bed called "The Dancing Angels" and a "Life Force Garden."

The otherworldly species in the S Bed can be identified by their markedly different vibrations, said Sheehan. She said that some old root stalks are growing new and different plants, and also that seeds dormant within the earth since the time of Atlantis are beginning to sprout.

But the garden that receives the most attention—and is most sought by the numerous visitors who come from all over the world—is the "Eight Garden." It is in the shape of a figure eight—the lemniscate, or symbol for infinity—and is at the cutting edge of connection with the fifth-dimension energies. "It symbolizes the cross-over point between something in manifestation and out of manifestation," said Sheehan. Thus, it provides a plan for ideas to take on form. Here, the Ascended Masters have anchored a "Violet Transmuting Flame," which, Sheehan explained, "is a cosmic gift which literally erases karma and negativity permanently."

Visitors invariably report feeling beneficent energies while in the Eight Garden. Anecdotal reports of healings have been attested to by some visitors as well.

In addition to guiding the garden work, the angel and elemental kingdoms have instructed Sheehan and her partners on how to make flower essences from their harvests. These are similar to Bach Flower Remedies—each one is designed to treat a specific physical, emotional, or spiritual condition or state. The essences have been changing and growing stronger in terms of energies every year, said Sheehan. Their emphasis has shifted away from addressing physical needs to what Sheehan terms the "ascension process," the uplifting and expansion of human consciousness.

Green Hope Farm is open to visitors during the summer. In addition, Sheehan lectures and teaches workshops.

She once thought that people who could talk to angels were special, but now knows that we can all learn to communicate and work with the angelic and elemental kingdoms. "Imagination is the bridge across," she said. "Things that we think are our imagination are really messages. The more attention I paid to the messages, the more I realized that we always channel—we are always connected."

Sheehan added that the partnership between realms is an exciting adventure for the angels and elementals, too.

Alycone Light Centre

Like Sheehan, Sylvia Schechter's psychic opening came through trauma. When she was seven years old, she suffered food poisoning and had a clinical death. In her near-death experience, she said, "the veil between worlds was dissolved, and I was able to see into other dimensions." Ever since then, Schechter has been blessed with the ability to perceive spirit presences on both the inner and outer planes. She helps people attune to their own angels and to the nature spirit kingdom.

In 1977, Sylvia and her husband, Lawrence, were guided to meditate on the slopes of Mt. Shasta. They were directed to a site sixty miles north, in the Colestin Valley, on the Oregon-Washington border, where they would then found the Alcyone Light Centre. They took the name Alcyone from the brightest star in the cluster Pleiades. "Light Centre," said Sylvia, connotes a lens or transducer for receiving high-potency energies, and for enlightenment.

Alcyone is now a 360-acre site with an emerging campus for people to experience healing, spiritual learning, and interdimensional communication. There are various ongoing workshops and projects aimed at spiritual growth, ecological balance, and living in harmony with the earth. "We work with knowledge from our past lives, and in total cooperation with all the kingdoms," said Schechter. The angelic/devic kingdoms provide guidance on planting and building.

Meanings

What can we learn from the devic and angelic presences? These gateways are part of a much larger picture, a great unfolding that is taking human consciousness to higher levels. Increasingly, we are penetrating other dimensions in experiences that give us a glimpse of a vast cosmic picture. Exploring these unknown realms requires a loving guidance. Our unconscious call for help has been answered in the manifestation of angels, devas, and elemental spirits. In particular, the nature-oriented beings, whom we call devas, elementals, and nature spirits, connect us to the souls of all things on the earth. It is a connection that much of the modern world has lost, and one that is needed in order for us to reach spiritual wholeness.

There is a personal perspective in this unfolding as well. Nobbs described it eloquently. "I have a sense of the continuance of all life," he said. "I am strongly aware of the spiritual world that underpins the physical world. This gives me a sense of detachment, that however dreadful things might get personally, it would not be the end of the story. I feel as if I can cope with anything."

Underground Kingdoms in Legend and Lore

Illustration by John O'Neil for *Ozma of Oz* by L. Frank Baum

The "Nome" King confronts a chicken.

Look Out Below!

David F. Godwin
January 2000

Perhaps an encounter between nomads and cave dwellers in prehistoric times gave rise to the notion of underground realms and their inhabitants. Or perhaps the phenomenon is some sort of psychological allegory of the unconscious mind. Or could it be...based on fact? In any case the belief has persisted from the earliest times that there are folks living *down there.*

In perhaps the earliest manifestation of this legend, many ancient peoples believed that the dead inhabited an underground kingdom ruled over by a deity such as the Greek Hades or the Norse goddess Hel. This concept seems to have reached its fullest realization in Dante's elaborate map of hell described in his *Inferno.*

There were other tales about dwellers underground that became widespread in the Middle Ages. Fairies and elves were said to inhabit strange worlds inside earthen mounds where revels were held on a continuous basis and time passed differently than in the outside world. Deep in the mines, gnomes and kobolds held sway and either helped or terrorized human miners. In our own times, L. Frank Baum wrote a number of Oz books featuring the "Nome King" and his underground empire of jewels, gems, caverns, and treasure-laden halls. (The spelling of "gnome" was simplified so as not to confuse the kiddies.) George MacDonald wrote about a similar empire of goblins threatening to take over a human kingdom in *The Princess and the Goblin.*

Eventually, these stories culminated in theories of a hollow earth. Seriously propounded by men such as John Cleves Symmes, William Reed, and Raymond W. Barnard, this idea received unforgettable fictional treatment by Edgar Rice Burroughs in his Pellucidar series, beginning with *At the Earth's Core* in 1922. Burroughs followed Jules Verne's example in inhabiting the inner regions of the earth with prehistoric creatures. Meanwhile, in the nineteenth century, Cyrus Teed was convinced that, not only is the earth hollow, but we live on the inside!

In 1871, Edward Bulwer-Lytton published *The Coming Race* wherein he told about a superior subterranean civilization with designs on the surface world. These people made free use of a mysterious force called vril—a source of energy considered to be a real phenomenon by Madame Blavatsky and others.

John Uri Lloyd wrote one of the stranger inner-world novels with *Etidorhpa* (1895). The tale is told to a character named Llewellyn Drury by an old man who calls himself simply "I-Am-The-Man-Who-Did-It." The story is much too involved to summarize here, but suffice it to say that I-Am-The-Man explores the inner earth and ultimately undergoes some sort of advanced spiritual initiation. Hint: *Etidorhpa* is "Aphrodite" spelled backwards.

In the realm of nonfiction, the painter Nicholas Roerich popularized the legend of the underground kingdom of Agharti, which lay beneath Asia and was ruled over by "the King of the World," a Messiah-like figure.

More recently, and perhaps more familiar to FATE readers, in 1945, Richard

Shaver began writing about the underground kingdom of the evil, saucer-piloting deros in *Amazing Stories.* According to Shaver, the deros are responsible for all the evils of mankind, including the rise of Hitler, the death of Franklin Roosevelt, the assassination of John F. Kennedy, and the Crucifixion of Jesus Christ. (Hitler, incidentally, is rumored to be still alive and to have a secret underground UFO base in Antarctica.) Shaver's material and an unprecedented reader response dominated the pages of the magazine until it stopped, suddenly and myteriously, in 1948. The reasons given by editor Ray Palmer all sounded rather lame. Maybe he was just tired of it. Maybe the deros got to him.

The legend of an underground kingdom inhabited by beings who do not necessarily have our best interests at heart persists in modern guise. A major part of ufology folklore involves a subterranean city in New Mexico—probably beneath Area 51—populated by extraterrestrials who perform genetic experiments on human subjects in exchange for alien technology. I haven't seen this techno-metropolis, but there are those who say they have.

Whatever the truth, humanity persists in believing that there is a lot more under our feet than mere dirt and stone.

drawing by Uldene Trippe, from *On the Road to Make Believe* by Frederick J. Forster (1924)

The Merry Nisse

These Scandinavian household spirits can be both frightening and helpful

Brad Steiger
March 2000

The night that I encountered "him" proved to be a life-altering event. The presence of this entity provided me with my personal proof of the reality of other dimensions of being, and set me on the quest that has dominated my life path.

That night, when I was a child of nearly five, I saw what is commonly referred to as an elf, a brownie—or, in the Scandinavian culture that is my heritage, a *nisse.* There are probably no cultures that do not have their own version of this often ancestral household spirit. Traditionally, Scandinavian families left a small portion of food out at night for the *nisse* to enjoy. I remember discussing the *nisse* with a friend in the Mesquaki (Fox) tribe, who said that they never forgot to leave an offering of food for their household spirit's evening nourishment.

Tricky Guardians

In the Scandinavian tradition, the *nisse* look after hearth and home, a kind of guardian entity—but one with an attitude. *Nisse* can be extremely volatile if provoked, and they are very often mischievous little tricksters. I have spoken to many folks who remember as children having their hair pulled, their toys hidden, their cat's tail pulled by the *nisse*. Although few of my friends admit to having seen *nisse*, a good many have strongly sensed their presence.

On that long-ago evening when I caught a *nisse* watching my parents, I believe that I suprised him as much as he did me, but he quickly regained his composure and gave me a strange kind of smile that was as benevolent as it was puckish. At the same time, I sensed that it was a conspiratorial kind of smile, as if we would forever share a secret that was profound in its simplicity.

I don't remember what happened after that, because his eyes suddenly became very compelling and seemed to grow larger and larger. And the next thing I knew, it was morning.

When I reported my experience to my parents, they were far more indulgent than one might suppose. According to my Danish mother's family tradition, we were in the lineage of Hans Christian Andersen and such encounters with the wee ones were not unexpected. Grandma Dena often spoke of the "pantry elf," another name for the *nisse*, and Grandma Anna reported seeing the entities as little bits of sparkling light.

As I have recounted my experience over the years, many listeners have expressed their opinions that I may actually have met an extraterrestrial alien—a "Grey"—or a ghost; but I suspect that I came face to face with a *nisse*. And although I have never seen such a creature again, I have never lacked for evidence of their presence in my home. And I must give full credit to my initial encounter with the being for my desire to learn more about the human psyche and our niche in the universe, and for my various psychic safaris to investigate a wide range of unexplained phenomena—from poltergeistic disturbances and haunted houses, to UFO manifestations and woodland monsters. Because of my childhood meeting with a *nisse*, I learned at an early age that our species is part of a larger community of intelligences, a far more complex hierarchy of powers and principalities—both seen and unseen, physical and nonphysical—than most of us are bold enough to believe.

Finer Points of Creature Lore

We must at this point make the distinction between *nisse* and trolls. Although a few years back some enterprising Danes made a fortune cleaning up the image of trolls and selling them to an unsuspecting public as cute little creatures with big bug-eyes, dolphin grins, and bushy red hair, real trolls are nasty buggers who can assume gigantic proportions and wreak havoc whenever they choose. To be even more precise, they are fiendish giants, very often associated with hostile, darkside sorcerers.

I have heard many an ill-informed salesperson refer to the benignly grinning troll dolls as Scandinavian elves or *nisse*. To be fair, however, among more contemporary and less traditional Danes there did develop a tendency to confuse the identity of the *huldrefolk* (elves often involved in changeling tales) with trolls, and to envision them as brownie-like beings. Though it is difficult to imagine how any entities involved in baby-napping could ever be considered cute and adorable.

Tiny Demons

I must admit, there have been times when I certainly didn't consider our *nisse* as charming and adorable, either. Once when I was a teenager, the *nisse* decided to terrorize me when I was home alone on the farm. It began with doors opening and closing of their own volition, terrible poundings on walls and windows, and the palpable sense of a menacing presence. Interestingly, our dog, Queen, a collie/wolf mix who took no nonsense from anyone or anything, also sensed—or may even have seen—the wild and crazy *nisse*. Her hair bristled, she bared her teeth, and she directed her warning growls at an unseen troublemaker. It was incredible to watch her attention being directed and redirected at various places in the house as the invisible entity moved from place to place, thudding walls and scattering books and papers.

Queen and I finally retreated upstairs, determined to make a brave last stand against our assailant. I will never forget kneeling with my .22 rifle, my faithful dog snarling at my side, awaiting the creature as it noisily ascended the stairs, step by step. Thankfully, before I could shoot any holes in the walls, there was a peculiar "whoosh" of air around us, a tiny sound of tinkling laughter, and the spooky game was over. Queen shook her head and whined in puzzlement, and I felt an overwhelming sense of relief that there really was no monster in the house about to rend us limb from limb. It had all been a merry prank played on me by the *nisse*.

As I considered the impetus for such an eerie demonstration, I recalled reading an issue of the great old pulp magazine *Weird Tales*, and my father remonstrating that such stories could pop back into my memory at the most inopportune times to frighten me. Of course I had scoffed at such an ill-founded paternal warning and laughed that a robust 15-year-old such as myself could not be easily frightened by anything. Almost as I had spoken those words, I sensed an unseen presence accepting the challenge.

Peaceful Coexistence

As I became an experienced investigator of psychical manifestations, I eventually encountered the gamut of eerie displays—spectral appearances, ghostly voices, and a seemingly inexhaustible range of poltergeist demonstrations. For the past many years, the activity of our household *nisse* are benignly mischievous. Most often, a book or file that I have had in plain sight on my desk will suddenly not be there when I reach for it. After a brief search to prove what I already know—that I have not misplaced the objects—I will say aloud, "All right, guys. Bring it back right now!" I might wait a couple of minutes before I leave the room to get a drink of water or to check on my wife Sherry, and when I return, the missing book or file has been returned to the center of my desk.

Sherry, who also enjoys Swedish heritage among her United Nations ancestry of French, Italian, Irish, and Chippewa, soon caught on to the games that *nisse* play. I will often hear her shouting out from her upstairs office, "Nisse! That's enough. Leave me alone now! Bring back my papers!"

In our household, we enjoy a very peaceful coexistence with the *nisse*. Some are obviously always concerned with our health and happiness and serve as guardians of our home. Others, well, they are a bit more fun-loving and will always delight in temporarily hiding objects that we had moments ago been using. Such behavior, though, is really not all that obnoxious. Annoying sometimes, yes, but, after all, the *nisse* keep our house from ever becoming the least bit boring!

The Wee People in My Backyard

Elves Were Her Friends

Sherry Hansen Steiger
March 2000

As far back as I can remember, they have always been there. Such an active part of my childhood, yet one that faded into the category of an active imagination—or was it? "They" were the wee people, my best friends and constant companions.

Grandma Johnson's backyard was full of lilac bushes, peonies, raspberry bushes, and toadstools. It was not only the majestic colors and heavenly fragrances that beckoned me to crawl amongst the overhanging, burgeoning branches (to my small stature, a private and cozy little world unto themselves)—it was the magic of my little playmates!

I lived at Grandma's until I was about eight years old. Each and every day the weather permitted me to play in the backyard, that was always my favorite place to be. My wee friends were seldom in the same place two days in a row. They loved to play hide and seek with me, and frequently would surprise me by peeking out from under a different flower or bush, from some hidden recess of the yard, or new vegetation I had not yet discovered.

As soon as I had wiped the sleep from my eyes, I would look out the window with hope and anticipation that the weather, and my grandma, would allow me to enter my magical world and its surprise inhabitants.

My mother has always told me I was "Nature's Child," as it was next to impossible to get me to come in the house, even to eat. I much preferred to eat outside—even sleep outside—if I could. Often, Grandma or Mom let me take my lunch outside, and I shared it with my friends. Sometimes I took breakfast crumbs out to them, putting them under what seemed to be a favored location—under the toadstools in the shade. Sometimes I would sit and wait, hoping the crumbs would lure them, but most often, they would lead me on a merry chase around the yard, hiding under a lilac branch, or even in a corner of the sandbox Papa built.

Grandma and Papa were from Sweden. They talked in Swedish when they didn't want me to know what was being discussed. I did hear the word "nissa," and many others that I couldn't prounounce, that seemed to be referencing my little friends. And little they were, not even as big as my little finger! Whenever I told Grandma or Papa of the tricks my friends had played on me—in hopes of luring them to the literal sight of the wee ones—the little people would disappear. I began to get the feeling that they would never show themselves to "big people."

It never entered my mind that other children didn't have their own wee people in their bushes and flowers, although I don't recall ever asking. These tiny elves favored nature and lived outdoors, (they seemed to have a secret entrance/ exit—into a tunnel located near several spots where the toadstools were most prevelant). But in the winter months they would appear at nighttime to tuck me into bed, after my prayers. They would pull the covers close to my neck and cuddle, for a few minutes, just until I would begin to fall asleep…then go back to their own kingdom.

Grandma's dad was a poet and songwriter in Sweden. One poem, that was probably not his, but which I heard Grandma recite frequently, was a scene familiar to my own, and perhaps explained why she was tolerant of my elf-mates: *Kvallens guldmoln fastet kransa, alvorna pa angen dansa, och den bladbekronta Nacken gigan ror i silverbacken.* The nearest English translation is: "The golden clouds of evening encircle the sky; the elves are dancing in the meadow and the leaf-crowned water sprite plays in the silvery brook."

To this very day, I cannot say if this was as real and physical as it seemed to me to be in my childhood. Perhaps the elves and fairies really do exist, as they are present in most every culture in some form, and may truly be a part of the many dimensions that are not always evident to the human eye and ear. Physicists say that we are only able to perceive a fraction of all frequencies that exist in and around us in the vast world of inner and outer space.

To me, all of Creation is miraculous and God's miracles and splendor just could possibly include that of elves!

drawing by Uldene Tripppe, from *On the Road to Make Believe* by Frederick J. Forster (1924)

Childish Things

Kids know what is real

Edain McCoy

March 2000

Do nature spirits exist? It's not a question I entertain for debate. I believe they do exist, and I accept their existence as part of the universe in which I live. But I admit that this was not always the case. Due to the imposition of our culture, I was true to the words of the Apostle Paul: "When I became an adult, I put away childish things." I shudder now at what this imperative almost cost me.

As a child, I had a firm belief in the world of nature spirits, or faeries as they are commonly called. I developed my notion of what they must look like from drawings in children's storybooks, though I don't know why I filtered out all the other fanciful creatures in those books, and locked on to faeries as the ones who were "real." I think I just knew what was true and what was not, because I was still young enough not to have yet been acculturated into accepting the version of reality of our larger society.

Even as a young tomboy, climbing trees and making mud creations in my backyard, I was aware of another world of beings who were always near me. This unseen world somehow overlapped my own, more solid reality, but still I knew it was there all around me. I never felt alone.

I was one of those kids who could be put to bed, but not made to sleep. Long after my parents retired for the night, hoping I had finally fallen asleep, I would sit in the window of my bedroom gazing at the two large trees on the front lawn. These trees always seemed alive, with a sentience all their own. I didn't know the word "dryad" (the name given to nature spirits who inhabit trees), but I would see their faces in my dreams of the trees, and I fretted for them during the fierce spring storms that routinely pound the Midwest.

That window also afforded me a panoramic view of our neighbor's English-style garden. I have always been drawn to its lush, colorful interior. To me it exuded enchantment, like an opening to another realm. Fearing I would damage the carefully tended space, I was warned by my mother to keep out.

One particularly sleepless night, I was sitting at the window watching the rich, golden glow of the full moon on the garden. The glow coalesced into a sparkling light, centralized around the bloom of a pale yellow rose. As I watched the sparkling closely, forms of human-like beings took shape. They were feminine beings, with flowing gowns that seemed to be one with their translucent bodies. They danced joyfully in a circle around the roses as if playing a game.

For a moment I thought I was seeing ghosts and was afraid. As I held my

from *Marchen und Sagen:Schatz* (Theo. Stroefer's Kunstverlag, 1885)

breath on the verge of a major shout, I realized these creatures were not ghosts. They simply did not bear enough resemblance to humans to be our spirit doubles. These creatures were small—about three feet high—and they had wings! The wings were quite large, but faint and ephemeral—almost like impressions of wings, rather than real ones. The creatures seemed to walk upon the ground, yet they seemed above it and a part of it all at the same time. I could not see through them, but the light of the moon passed through them as if they were not there at all, and they left no shadow. Their arms moved gracefully, almost blending with the air through which they swept, and I sensed rather than heard their musical sound that I likened to laughter.

I couldn't tear my eyes from the wonderful scene. I sank down in the window, fearing that if I was seen, the beings would go away. I wanted to keep watching them. I wanted to go out and dance with them. I wanted to be them. I don't remember how the event ended, but I awoke in my own bed the next morning, having been placed there by my father. I chattered out my experiences to my parents at breakfast expecting, in my childish innocence, that they would share my excitement. Their verdict? I was dreaming. There were no such things as faeries. They laughed—it was cute, they thought. They dismissed my conversation and went on to discuss other matters, leaving me with the vague sense that I had said or done something that would have been unacceptable if I was their age and not a child.

I tried to believe them. After all, they were adults. They knew about things I didn't. If they said there were no faeries, then it must be true. Yet I found myself pining to have entry again to the faery world. For months I felt an acute longing for those creatures and their realm—just as the ancient legends tell us will happen once their world is opened to us.

The pressure of society's worldview won out in the end. In fact, I had almost forgotten my faery experience altogether when my grandmother gave me a very special children's storybook as an Easter present the following spring. I was delighted to find it contained many poems and drawings about faeries. As I leafed through the book exclaiming my delight, I came upon a page that made me stop short. There was a poem about faeries dancing in a moonlit garden, and the drawing that accompanied the poem displayed a clear image of exactly the creatures I had seen almost a year ago in my neighbor's garden.

I was thrilled to know that at least one other person somewhere in the world had seen what I had and knew it to be real. But I hugged that knowledge to myself, instinctively knowing it was better for me to keep this secret between me and the artist of the book. Though I did not have the maturity to analyze this coincidence too deeply, I silently began to question the truth I had been taught.

Children Grow Up

Like all children, I grew up, and even the most spellbinding events and

In 1920, Frances Griffiths and Elsie Wright created a sensation by claiming to have photographed fairies. The "fairies" later proved to be drawings cut out of fairy books, but the girls always maintained that they had really seen fairies despite faking the photographs.

games of childhood's days fell behind me. I don't think I stopped believing in faeries. I just didn't think about them anymore, as my mind turned to the allure of stylish clothing, makeup, boys, parties, and all the joys and trials of a teenage girl.

Then, at age 16, my worldview took a turn backward. I was with my father in a used bookstore, and I found a book called *The Grimoire of Lady Sheba*. This was a book on the basic beliefs of a nature religion, labeled "evil" by its detractors. I was fascinated by the concept and persuaded my father to buy it for me. That book pointed the way down a path that would lead me, seven years later, to seriously study and become initiated into an ancient religion that venerates the whole of nature.

I realized nature spirits existed, as surely as I had once believed they did, and that those faeries I viewed from the bedroom window of my childhood has been just as real as myself. Empowered by this realization, I launched a quest to learn all I could about the world's faery lore. I started gathering information on nature spirits with the zeal of a half-starved squirrel packing away nuts for winter. Then I did the hardest thing I ever set out to do. I was determined to consciously reconnect with the world of nature spirits, and to interact with them as our ancestors had once done quite normally.

Like memories of our past lives and of the God with whom we dwelt before our births, memories of faeries fade rapidly if they are not kept alive. Nature spirits recede from us as we grow up, and they are loath to renew that contact. They know we are taught to dismiss our early memories. They are aware of the attitude of adults toward their lore and, most deplorable, that we are responsible for mass destruction of much of our world's natural resources. These resources are their homes, and channels for them to contact us. As natural places are destroyed, so is a large portion of their world and its inhabitants.

Against these odds I persevered, and eventually regained the connection I dearly wish now had never been severed. I wanted to share that information with others. In 1994 Llewellyn published my book, *A Witch's Guide To Faery Folk*. To my surprise and delight, the appeal of that book goes far beyond those who follow nature religions. Since its publication, I have received letters from teens and adults all over the world who relate their childhood experiences with beings they now know to be faeries.

These writers are Lutheran, Catholic, Jewish, agnostic, and Quaker. They are from all cultures and economic backgrounds. They are well-educated professionals and from the working classes. Like me, they were told that faeries were foolishness or imagination, and they allowed themselves to be shamed into silence and forgetfulness.

The nature spirits of the world are our living connection to the life force of the planet that sustains us. Keeping alive a connection to them makes us realize that nature is alive and should be respected and preserved. Whether we like to think about it or not, we all know this to be true. If nature and her spirits die, humanity will die with them. But we continue to destroy nature with a callous nonchalance, seemingly unconcerned with the consequences of our actions. Only reaffirming our faith in our childhood beliefs in nature spirits will teach us this lesson of our interdependence upon nature before its too late.

Almost a century ago the great British author J. M. Barrie penned the classic tale of Peter Pan, a mortal boy who does not want to grow up and lose his connection with the enchanted world. He instinctively knows that if he allows himself to slip into adulthood, this realm will be taken from him by the culture in which adults dwell. As the life-light of his faery friend Tinkerbell begins to fail, Peter and his friends save her with their belief. Truly, something within these special beings dies when humankind ceases to believe.

Believe and accept. The spirits of nature are with us always, and they will gladly make themselves known to us if we open our senses to them without censor—as we did before we "put away childish things."

Devas, Elves, and Us

Nature Spirits at Findhorn

drawings by Marko Pogacnik, from *Nature Spirits and Elemental Beings* (Findhorn Press, 1996)

Lettuce deva in Marko Pogacnik's garden in Slovenia

Tony Mitton
March 2000

Appropriately, it was a little child, my unborn son, who led me into the world of nature spirits. My partner and I, both British and living in Spain, were discussing where he should be born, to avoid the hazards of dual nationality. We had just read *The Secret Life of Plants* by Peter Tompkins, and were impressed with its account of the Findhorn Community and their cooperation with the subtle realms of Nature. It seemed an exciting place, on the cutting edge of spiritual exploration. They had no guru and professed no dogma, nor did they ask for all your money before admitting you, all of which we found reassuring. Almost without discussion, it became plain to us that Findhorn was where we should go.

We arrived with no other expectation than that we would stay. After some hesitation the Community agreed, mainly because my partner had worked for many years in hotel management and they had just acquired Cluny Hill, a large hotel. It was typical of Findhorn's divine logic that she never worked a day at Cluny, though she lived in the Community for twenty years!

We had not been at Findhorn for more than a couple of days before we began to learn about nature spirits. We were told that there are two distinct orders. The first was contacted by cofounder Dorothy Maclean in Findhorn's early days. They were called "devas" which means "shining ones." Devas are an order of angelic being whose purpose is to focus and maintain the form of each specific plant species, ensuring that the seed will reproduce in the same configuration as the parent plant. Devas are very powerful, but only within the constrained limits of their purpose.

The devas had not experienced modern humans with whom they could communicate and there was mutual surprise at the contact. One senses excitement, curiosity and a desire to experiment. Since Peter Caddy, another cofounder, had started a garden to supplement the family diet (they were living on welfare at the time), the obvious focus was on vegetables. The ground was so sandy that Peter had intended to plant only lettuce and radishes, but the devas told Dorothy that they had power to change the very constitution of the soil. She received very specific instructions on where and when to plant, what compost to apply, and so on, all of which Peter obeyed faithfully. The results were astounding. Vegetables grew so prolifically and to such size and lusciousness that they attracted attention not only from the locals who bought the surplus, but from the far corners of Britain. The prize example was a 40-pound cabbage. Unwilling to be thought a crank, Peter maintained for a while that good compost was all it took. However, after the Soil Association had conducted tests and found little in the garden to distinguish it from the surrounding sand dunes, he finally admitted to the participation of the devas.

These results, which could properly be called miraculous, could not have been achieved without the participation of the second order of nature spirits, the earth elementals whom we know, or used to know, under their folk names of elf, gnome, fairy, pixie, goblin, and so on. These elementals put the devas' instructions into practice, working on the constitution of the soil, nurturing the life force in the seed, overseeing the development of bud and flower and finally attending to the process of decay, seeding, and recycling. In human terms, the devas are the architects who develop a blueprint, and the elementals the masons, carpenters, and expert artisans who bring it to physical reality.

A goblin by the fireside at the inn at Dölach, Carinthia

Four Dimensions

We can better understand the two orders of nature spirits if we view the human being as a composite of physical, etheric, astral and spiritual dimensions. We are the only beings on the planet to combine all four; we share the etheric or life level with the elementals and the astral or emotional/mental level with the angels, who include the devas. It is because we share the etheric and astral dimensions with the elementals and the angels respectively that we are able to communicate with them. Indeed, we each have our own specific elemental and angel, the elemental driving our physiological functions and the angel dwelling in our mind and feelings. In the levels natural to them, these beings live in a state of love and joy. Human beings are something of a mystery to them, because, despite our obviously greater potential, we so often exhibit the contrary qualities.

Evolution is a universal process, and the angelic and elemental realms are each engaged on their own paths. These paths are separate but linked with each other and with our own. Each realm has its own hierarchy, though this is often misconceived as a top/down arrangement on the human model.

Rather, each rank of a hierarchy is essential to the rest. For example, angels are concerned in the lives of individual humans. It is because of their work that the higher orders, archangels, principalities, and powers, can do theirs, which is to guide nations, influence the *zeitgeist,* and inspire change. Though, of course, angels only inspire ideas and indicate opportunities, and never presume to interfere with human free will.

Among elementals there is a similar hierarchy which ranges from the sprites working with the growth stages of individual plants and the constituents of the soil, elves, fairies, and gnomes; through those who care for the character of a particular area, holding in their consciousness the work of all the myriad elementals within it; to the august Lord of All, the great god Pan. His name means "All Things." Pan was held by the ancient Greeks to be the consciousness of all that lives and grows upon the planet. One detects his presence by a certain frisson which starts at the nape of the neck and descends the back to invade the body, hence our word "panic." Despite this, his presence is loving and his touch is gentle. Marko Pogacnik's groundbreaking book, *Nature Spirits and Elemental Beings,* tells of meetings with Pan, as does Peter Caddy's autobiography, *In Perfect Timing.* R. Ogilvie Crombie (Roc) has also presented an intimate portrait in an audio-visual which was shown at Findhorn while I was there.

Communication

Humans communicate with angels relatively easily, perhaps because both can operate at a mental level. Communication with the elementals is more difficult because they operate entirely through feelings. Our thoughts are incomprehensible, at least to the lower ranks of their hierarchy. Though they are well aware of our feelings and activity, they make no judgments. They are closely bound to particular locales and when we work against them, which may happen when we develop suburbs, build motorways, or even lay out our gardens, they simply endure and wait. I know of few occasions when they strike back, but they may cease their activity and then the land will sicken.

Every nature elemental is part of the universal consciousness of Earth, the Mother revered from ancient times. If, for example, you feel drawn to a particular tree, perhaps for the strength of its branches or the elegance of its form, you may learn much if you open your heart and meditate beside it. After a while you may pose a question and let the responsive images flow uncritically into your mind. You may interpret them for your own understanding and even ask for clarification if they seem obscure, but it is necessary to keep your heart open and loving and your thoughts positive and under strict control, eliminating arrogance and ego.

Pan revealing himself in the guise of the Celtic god Cernunnos

By the time my partner and I arrived at Findhorn, the giant vegetables were only a memory. A decision had been taken, one imagines at the highest level, to grow people rather than vegetables. Obviously this had relevance to the birth of Aquarius and the new consciousness, which Peter Caddy assured us was already with us. But I think there was another, more pressing, reason. Peter's admission about the source of the garden's fecundity had attracted publicity, and people had been arriving, anxious to believe. Some had stayed to form the beginnings of the Community. However, the average human, inheritor of karma which is usually unresolved, presents negative aspects which the pure, clear consciousness of elementals finds hard to tolerate. Contact becomes difficult for them, even painful.

During my time at Findhorn, the realm of nature spirits was a substrate to our life, the basis from which we developed our activities in the various work departments. The gardeners worked with them and artists made sketches, but for most of us they were a given, like the ground we walked on. I spent much time in the Maintenance Department and there I encountered the elementals of machines. These reflect the emotional states of the people who made them; a possible explanation for those "lemon" automobiles. However, they are our human responsibility, not Earth's. My most memorable encounter with Nature's elementals occurred when, for the first time in years, I took time off to do as I liked. I went alone to the west of Scotland, a magical land of mist and moor, deep lakes and tall hills, and wound up on the Isle of Skye, fabled in legend and history. I became depressed as I crossed the interior of the island, for it was just a flat expanse of peat bog, treeless and barren save for clumps of dry, tussocky grass. The "Brown Lands" in Tolkien's *Lord of the Rings* might have presented just such an aspect. Where were the elves and pixies, I wondered. I had been so sure I would find them here. Two days later my wanderings took me to Dunvegan Castle, home of the Fairy Flag. I had no sooner entered the grounds when my inner ear heard a joyous shout, "Here we are!" Around me I sensed the missing elves and fairies to the number of perhaps 400, all smiling and laughing. I learned afterward that the lord of the castle, Chief of Clan McLeod, had hired an expert gardener to embellish and re-invigorate the grounds. I concluded that the elementals of the island had migrated *en masse* to a place where they could be useful—and therefore happy.

The same trip afforded me another glimpse into the interaction between humans and the subtle realms of Earth. I was taking a long walk over rough and barren country between two seacoasts. A wild gale was blowing off the Atlantic and visions kept recurring of brown cloaked, red-skirted women working in fields where dun-colored cattle grazed beside homesteads, all nestled beneath a little fortress on a hill. But there was nothing there, neither women nor cattle nor even fields, though worn-down earthen banks attested to their one-time presence. I climbed the hill to find ruins of a fort. A simple test convinced me that what I was seeing was, at some level, real. I concluded that the consciousness of the land, sickened of its barren and untended state, was resting in a past time when humans had cared for and worked with it. In his book, *Healing the Heart of the Earth*, Marko Pogacnik warns of the damage we do by neglecting the elemental realms. In our ignorance we often destroy the sacred sites where in past times priests and priestesses worked with the powers of Earth for mutual reinforcement and sustenance. Though the environmental movement represents an advance in human consciousness, it is wholly geared to human survival and gives no consideration to the real needs of Earth. We are like a husband who thinks his wife should be satisfied with the housekeeping money and offers her no affection or tenderness.

It is my belief that words like "elf," "fairy," and "angel" are not the inventions of superstition but the observations of an old perception, decayed but in the process of re-establishing itself. Such words occur in every culture, past and present. My own experience, and that of many others, is that our intellect, whose expression is judgmental, analytical, and egotistic, is the enemy of our former perceptiveness, which was loving and holistic. It is only gradually that intellect has become dominant, so that we have come to see consciousness as centered in the brain. I do not suggest that we should abandon intellect, won with such sacrifice, but simply that we should not let it rule us. If we can join heart consciousness to head consciousness, we will empathize better with our fellows and may obtain a broader perspective on our world. Synchronistically, medical research is finding that some heart transplant patients remember events from the life of the dead donor, a person they never knew. In his scholarly work, *The Heart's Code*, Paul Pearsall concludes that there are centers of consciousness outside the brain.

Working With the Earth

In the past, humans worked with the forces of Earth to invigorate and enhance their mutual life. The ancient religions were dedicated to this goal, celebrating their sacred rituals within stone circles and around earthen mounds. It must be admitted however that there was a shadow side—

attempts by evil men and women to wrest the subtle powers out of their proper paths and use them for personal ends. Despite all, the nature spirits send a clear message: there is no judgment, no purposed revenge for past or present errors. We need to forgive ourselves and press forward to the new challenge. This is the evolutionary quantum leap which is now upon us. Human beings ARE growing, witness Mandela, de Klerk, and Gorbachev. Peace has become a constant word on our lips. The cycle of time is beckoning us to a new plateau on our evolutionary path. No one is to be left behind. Marko Pogacnik's book, *Christ Power and the Earth Goddess*, quotes messages from the Archangel Michael. He urges us to bestir ourselves and take this evolutionary step jointly with the hierarchy of angels and Earth and its nature spirits. Our past has been linked with them and this should continue into the future. It is my hope that on that new plateau we shall all mingle in joy and clear consciousness, to grow and go forward together.

A fairy gift

Green Nature Spirits

Ann Moura
March 2000

I learned my Green Craft from my mother, as she had learned from hers. Common throughout our generations is the custom of setting a bowl of milk outside the back door on nights of the Full Moon for the Fair Folk.

As I grew older, married, and raised my family, we have continued the tradition, but frequently with a slight twist—a bowl of whiskey seems to hit the spot for the Fairies on chilly nights! Sometimes, as I reach for the milk, a gentle, whimsical voice echoes in my ear, "Have you nothing a little stronger?" Then, I feel a tug towards a bottle of wine on the refrigerator shelf, or the impression comes to me of how much better a bit of blackberry brandy or Irish Mist would look in the ritual bowl. The following day, we are often thrilled to find a Fairy Ring of mushrooms near the bowl—we know they partied hearty under the moonlight!

I like to leave my gift on a piece of driftwood under the elder tree at the edge of the garden. This graceful chunk of wood has been my Fairy Altar for over fifteen years. It is decorated with a musical wind chime suspended from one point of the bare, antler-like branch that arches over the base. On the ground at one side of the altar I keep a bowl of imported Irish shamrocks which seem to be in perpetual bloom with delicate white flowers. These flowers are Fairy occupied, and they greet me cheerfully whenever I visit the garden. The flowers have trustingly kept me company for 14 years.

Why do I say, "trustingly"? My pot of Irish shamrocks have let me know by the sensations of their auras and their pretty smiles that they put their trust in me to keep them safely—as when we travelled cross-country and had to pass through a state that demands the extinction of all outside vegetation at its borders. The flowers, set on the floor of my car, turned their snowy faces up to me with worry and hope mingled in their auras. I told them to exude a shield and I would slip a scarf over them. We passed the checkpoint unchallenged by the person peering into my car while quizzing me on plants, fruit, and other forbidden vegetation. Since "Fairies" were not on the prohibited list, I was quite secure in shaking my head in the negative.

Do I talk to the herbs and plants in my garden and yard? But of course! And when I am preoccupied, rosemary and artemesia extend their shrubby branches to me in sweet-scented consolation. A couple of times I have let the garden go a bit when I was too engrossed with my work to get to it. But each time I made the effort to tend the plants, I have the next day found a single feather laid at my doorstep, so I know the Fairies appreciated my work. Betony, on the other hand, giggles at me shamelessly as I lift it and its long white trailing root from the soft soil of the flower bed and deposit it in a barren portion of the yard. Betony and I both know the joke—it will root where it lands and spread anew. Now it fills the area under some trees and shrubs, adding color and texture where previously the ground was bare.

Fairies, Devas, and Sprites are names for the spirit energies of plants, stones, crystals, or springs, and if you open yourself to living Nature, these essences will reveal their hidden selves to you. They occupy plants, for example, but are

Shamrock fairies on kitchen sill.

not confined to them, and will occasionally depart to frolic together—some favoring the Full Moon, others the Dark Moon. I was smitten by the beauty of Fairies as a child in Colorado (decades before Colorado became "fashionable"), when I encountered a field full of pale blue and white wild columbines. Their Fairy hosts danced and waved, laughed and teased, and I was utterly charmed by their grace and spontaneity. Their slim, lithe forms were only one to two inches tall, blending in perfectly with the flowers they inhabited, and attired with little caps that matched their short, petally skirts.

Some plants take a little longer than others to be communicative. You have to consider their past. Was it raised by a landscape company or nursery? If so, the energy may be confused by the comings and goings of plant friends until settled into a new home. Was it threatened by builders? Have people abused it? Trees especially have long memories about these things. Their experiences are literally part of them, as anyone who knows how to read tree rings can affirm, so you should approach trees gently, and let them know you care. You can, for example, poke fertilizer spikes in the ground around their roots, water them regularly, and decorate them with a ribbon-trimmed charm or a wind chime (but nothing jarringly clanky).

With Circle Casting in the Craft, the besom (broom) is used to sweep out negativity from the space. I generally say something like, "I sweep from this space negativity and chaotic energies that they not manifest within my Circle." But I don't "banish" these energies as we need the balance and creative impulse they inspire. Once I was conducting a class in the Green Craft to which a mother had included her middle-school age son. As I swept the Circle with an oak sprig I had picked up nearby, I spied a little entity watching me from beside the boy. This was a light green Fairy with spiky, ragged edges who gave me a forlorn look of "Do I hafta go?" I sensed at once a youthful bit of chaos energy who felt drawn to the boy. All this took place in an instant, so I modified my wording at once with "…except for the little chaos energy by (name)." The entity grinned with delight at being included within the Circle, but I think some of the students thought I was a bit daft.

It was during the Cakes and Wine simple feast, as I was demonstrating the symbolic Great Rite with cup and athame, that an adult student with prior Craft training interrupted with an offhand quip, but he instantly silenced. I continued on, noticing only that he had an unusual expression on his face. At the end of the class, he apologized for his ill-timed remark. He explained that the moment he spoke, he was startled to see a flash of green light fly across the circle, right up to his face, and glare at him. Instantly, it returned to the side of the boy, and the man knew he had been chastised. Until the ritual ended, he said nothing more.

As you can see, Fairies take their duties very seriously, so when you want to ensure privacy for a ritual, take a twig of straw and wave it through the air outside: "I call upon thee Fair Ones, that one of you take up residence in this straw, to keep intruders away as I conduct my rite." Then lay the straw on the floor indoors, just in front of the entrance. When the ritual is over, wave the straw in the air outdoors again: "Bright blessings I give to you as you go in peace back to your dwelling, that we may ever be good neighbors, one to the other. So Mote It Be." Let the straw float away on a breeze or settle onto the ground by plants.

I was taught that if you want to work with the Fairy Folk, you should avoid having scotch broom around as they find the musty odor offensive. And what about asking an entity to depart? The boy's chaos companion did generate mischief for a while, so I let him and his mother know that a companion called can always be farewelled: "Gentle spirit, you have brought me joy and pleasure with your company. My blessings I give unto you to carry with you on your journey. Depart in peace and blessed be."

Nature spirits vary in tone and appearance according to the natural object they enliven. My elder tree was a skinny little sapling twig when I spotted it on the edge of a field being torn up for a housing development. With my husband to help me, we told the elder our intention to carry it away to a new, safe home. It looked shivery and nervous, but I talked to the sapling all the way home, hoping to soothe it. Once the sapling was planted and watered, the little elder appeared to be taking in her new surroundings (yes, definitely female!) at the end of the herb garden, with tropical trees and palmettos close by. We had moved these plants, too, from our previous house and they were doing very well, so perhaps they gave a good account of us to her. In a very short time the elder was growing, blooming, and offering me clusters of her tiny white flowers for tea. Birds came and gorged on her dark berries, and she grew larger. One day, Elder's aura seemed maternal to me, and searching around, I found her children. Two young shoots grew close by from her spreading roots, nestled by her foliage. I asked her if I could transplant them so they might grow better, and her aura softened with her consent. Over the years we have transplanted several of her children, and even her grandchildren. She is now matronly in appearance, her aura serene and loving, and it is at her roots that I placed my Fairy Altar of driftwood with the bowl of shamrocks alongside.

Nature Spirits—Their Intelligence & Form

Lily Hill Farm flower garden.

Penny Kelly
March 2000

We wanted to dig a pond in the southeast corner of our farm. We had heard that it was bad luck to move rocks or earth without informing the local nature spirits of your intent. Wiser yet was to ask permission, and wait for a sign that their permission was granted. There was already one pond, in the northwest corner of the farm, which had been there when we bought the place. One Sunday afternoon in late September, I walked out to this pond, sat down on the thick carpet of spruce needles along the shore, and tried to compose a message to the local landscape deva, or any of the nature spirits concerned with the care of the earth.

The effort to communicate was not going very smoothly. I wasn't sure who or what to address, or how to ask for such a permission. Part of me felt I had every right to do whatever I wanted, yet another part of me felt that asking to dig up the earth where some intelligent-but-invisible being might be living was an outrageous imposition. Also, I was completely uncertain of my ability to hear the answer that might come to me. What if I just heard what I wanted to hear?

I sat in the fading afternoon light, my mind addressing the request, listening for a response, then wandering off into other thoughts again and again. Eventually, I decided that perhaps the enjoyment of the pond, the towering spruce trees that surrounded it, and the warm afternoon air might be the extent of my success for the day. I continued to sit there for awhile, gazing across the water, when two shining forms took shape in midair.

One was a little above and to the right of the other, and both were stunning in beauty—regal in appearance, with a variety of shimmering lights making up their transparent forms. I could easily discern their faces. They had large, translucent eyes, and hands that seemed to emit waves of light. The rest of the form was composed of jewel-like colors arranged in what seemed to be robes. Or perhaps the robes composed the "body," each decorated with unique designs of complex, anthropomorphic figures. Brilliant vortices of light swirled around their heads, giving the appearance of flames, clouds of color, and even horn-like projections, with flowery shapes woven among these. For a minute I wondered if I was looking at a couple of devils, but they were so exquisitely beautiful and peaceful, with such an aura of power that I ended up staring, my heart pounding, as I wondered who they could be.

Conversation With Shining Beings

After deliberately looking away several times, and finding them still present, it occurred to me that perhaps these were the nature spirits to whom I had been calling. I had been hoping that I might hear some kind of answer to my request—this vision was much more than I had ever imagined.

After I finally calmed down a bit, I introduced myself and told the beings that my husband and I wanted to dig a pond, but wanted the permission of the nature spirits, or the landscape deva, or someone from the realm of subtle elementals before we started digging. I started to explain that we really wanted the pond, yet wanted the nature spirits to understand that we were

The fish pond.

trying to work with them, that we cared about what they thought. Then I started worrying that they might say no because we were just being selfish, or that I was telling them what I wanted instead of asking for permission, when it dawned on me that they already understood our intent or they would not have shown up. So I stopped, uncertain as to how to proceed.

They asked why we wanted a pond in that particular place. I told them that we liked water, wanted something to swim in, and thought it would add to the beauty of the landscape for us as well as a number of birds and animals.

They told me that we could go ahead and dig the pond, but we might have difficulty filling it. I acknowledged this, then couldn't think of anything else to say. I was still feeling overwhelmed at the vision that hung suspended before me. After a minute or two, still uncertain about what to say next, I stammered, "Are you sure it's okay?"

The answer was the same as before: "Yes, go ahead and dig your pond, but you will have difficulty filling it." Some time later the beings faded away.

I went back to the house and told my husband, Jim, of the encounter. With great enthusiasm he went ahead with the plans and the contract to dig the pond. We agreed that it was disappointing to think that we might dig the pond, and then have to wait a couple of years before it finally filled up, but we held onto the idea that soon we would be able to sit at our kitchen table and look out at sparkling summer water, or sit on the deck and gaze at the moonlight dancing across the pond's dark surface.

Willow Pond, as we named it, was finally dug in November of 1994. As I write these words, it is December of 1999, five years later, and there is still no more than two or three feet of water in the bottom of what was supposed to be a ten-foot deep pond. The birds and animals that share the farm with us love it, but we cannot see the surface of the water from the house or the yard. It is clear to us now that this pond is never going to fill up naturally. We will have to seal it with clay, then pump it full, and perhaps keep pumping. Of course, as the two shimmering devas indicated, this makes the whole project more difficult.

Voices of Nature

Aside from the fact that they were right in their assessment of the task, the experience of that particular day remains as vivid as if it happened a moment ago. For me it was a turning point. I had been working with a group of elves in our vineyards, but they appeared almost as small-scale versions of people—solid, dressed in mismatched clothing, with a variety of moods, activities, and goals. I had tried to contact devas, and heard an answer or two in my head. But this was different. This was truly a gift of vision from what I came to call the "Landscape Deva" (since that was who I had tried to contact), and another deva for whom I had no name. Together, they left me with the memory of a powerful presence at work in the land, and a sense of being dedicated to the service of life.

Since then, I have been privileged to see a variety of devas and nature spirits. I can only guess, but it appears that they exist as the intelligent expression of the energies of a substance, for instance, water or roses, wind or pine trees, and that they will communicate if they are approached. In the same way that each human is an intelligent spirit inhabiting a physical body, and is responsible for taking care of it, there is an intelligent spirit in each flower, each tree, each river or rock. Nature spirits spend their time taking care of their physical forms much as we do. Like us, they create a variety of experiences in the process. In fact, their creative ability to rebound in the face of humanity's dull inattention and destructive effects on the varieties of intelligent life teeming around them is remarkable. But their tolerance does have its limits, and for this reason many nature spirits are making an concerted effort to communicate from their side of life.

Are we listening? Are we getting any closer to the open, practical awareness that Nature is not there for us to conquer, and that doing so will do us in? It's hard to say. If such an awareness is growing, it remains for us to take action—to clean things up, institute new ways of feeding and sheltering ourselves, and cut back on our numbers. Of course, knowing what to do is one thing, and doing it is something else altogether. Perhaps awareness of nature spirits will grow naturally as we develop a greater sensitivity to life and Nature as a whole.

As my friend Alvey (a nature spirit) has said many times, "The foundation of yer reality is nature. Mine, too! We all come from the world of nature. Lose that direct connection and ye will lose the whole reality."

Alvey

Gary Morris, *New Zealand Landscapes* (Zedcor, 1997)

Nature Spirits of New Zealand

Richard Webster
March 2000

The Maori people of New Zealand have a highly involved cosmogony. They believe that for aeons of time Rangi (the sky) and Papa (the Earth) clung so tightly to each other that there was no light, and darkness filled the world. Finally, when their children managed to force them apart, the natural world began. Every plant and animal is descended from its ancestral parents, Rangi and Papa. The world is full of *atua*, or spirits. These spirit-gods played an important part in everyday life. Much of the time they were feared, but they were also a source of protection. In fact, there were evil spirits (*atua whiro*) as well as harmless ones. Although they were referred to as "spirit-gods," they were

Madeleine Orban-Szontagh, *Traditional Animals, Designs and Motifs* (Dover, 1996)

not worshipped. The arrangement was a straightforward one in which the people tried to placate the *atua* with offerings and charms, and in return, the *atua* would help them whenever possible. The beneficial spirits often lived in trees and other natural objects, and were usually invisible. Many *atua* served as guardians of *tapu* (sacred) places. Others served as spirit guardians, and looked after people, protecting them from harm and warning them of danger.

Nature spirits were particularly fond of water. Para-whenuamea, Hine-moana, Wainui and Te Ihorangi were *atua* representing water, the ocean, rain and mist. They were all called upon when necessary to help the people. The number of nature spirits was huge, and the spirits of the forests and seashore had to be thanked before hunting or harvesting began. This was done by reciting *karakia* (prayers).

The *patupaiarehe*, also known as fairies or nature spirits, are believed to live in large fortified villages on the tops of mist-covered hills. They come out only at night or on overcast and foggy days. They look very much like normal people. They are pale in color, have fair or reddish hair, eat their food raw, love music and wear exotic white clothing. Their ability on the flute is famous, as it has a magical effect on young women who are lured by the sweet music into their homes, seldom to be seen again.

Before the white man came to New Zealand, the *patupaiarehe* must have seemed terrifying with their fair hair, pale skin, and white clothes. Fortunately, there were remedies that the Maoris could use against them. These were cooked food, red ochre (a sacred color to the Maori), and fire. Although the *patupaiarehe* are often seen as hostile, they frequently showed friendliness towards the Maori people and even helped them at times. They have gained a bad reputation because of their love for young Maori women.

Maori figure carving.

William Allan Neilson, ed., *Webster's New International Dictionary, Second Edition, Unabridged* (G. and C. Merriam, 1944)

They are seldom seen but often heard. While walking in the Waitakere and Hunua Ranges, close to where I live in Auckland, I have often heard the *patupaiarehe* talking. You can hear their chatter clearly, but it is difficult to make out individual words. It is said that if you see the *patupaiarehe* you will immediately forget everything about your present life, until some accident brings it back, possibly years later.

In pre-European times, a Maori leader called Te Kanawa encountered the *patupaiarehe* while he and his men were out hunting kiwi one night. Even though they were close to the safety of their campfire they were terrified when they heard the sounds of a large group of approaching spirits. The spirits talked amongst themselves as they approached, and the men could discern the voices of men, women, and children. They came as close to Te Kanawa as they dared, retreating every time the fire was revived by the breeze.

The *patupaiarehe* were angry because Te Kanawa and his men were hunting on their hilltop. As soon as he realized this, Te Kanawa removed the greenstone tiki he wore around his neck and his ear pendants, one made of greenstone and the other of sharkstooth. He placed a stick in the ground and placed the three items on it. The spirits were fascinated with them and they all took a turn to handle and feel them. In the process, the *patupaiarehe* took the shapes and forms of these pendants, and then disappeared leaving the originals behind. By doing this, Te Kanawa placated the spirits and in the morning, he and his men went back down the mountain and never went hunting there again.

It is believed that the Maoris learned the secret of making fishing nets from the *patapaiarehe.* A man called Kahu-kura saw the spirits fishing one night, and joined them in pulling in their large seine net. As he was pale in complexion, the spirits did not notice him until daylight came. In early dawn the nets were pulled in. The spirits, unlike people, did not share the fish, but simply took the ones they wanted and strung them on a cord. Kahu-kura followed suit, but tied his fish on with a slipknot so that the fish kept falling off. The spirits kept telling him to hurry up and went to help him, but he kept on tying slipknots to keep the spirits occupied. Finally it became light enough for the spirits to see that Kahu-kura was not one of them. They fled, leaving the fish and the net behind. Kahu-kura took the net home and taught his children how to make them.

The Maoris also learned the secrets of weaving and other textile work from the *patupaiarehe.* According to legend, a young *patupaiarehe* maiden called Hine-Rehia was captured by a Maori chief while gathering seaweed. He married her and they had a large family. Hine-Rehia was talented at textile work, but, following the *patupaiarehe* tradition, worked at it only at night or on foggy and misty days. Consequently, the other women were unable to see what she was doing and learn from it. They appealed to a *tohunga* (priest) to put a spell on Hine-Rehia, so that she would be unable to distinguish night from day. This he did, and Hine-Rehia worked on through the day, while the womenfolk watched and learned. Finally, when Hine-Rehia tired and put away her work, she discovered the trick that had been played on her. She sang an incantation which brought down a fog which carried her away. As she disappeared, her husband and children heard her calling out a sad farewell. Even today, the Maori people cover up any handiwork they are working on at night and do not uncover it again until the sun has risen the next day. This is because they are scared that their amazing skill in textile work will be stolen back by the *patupaiarehe* and lost for ever.

There are also elves or sprites who act as guardians to the forest. They are known as *Te Tini-o-te-hakuturi* and are more similar to the nature spirits of the West than the *patupaiarehe.* They protect the trees in the forests. They also taught the art of carving to the Maoris. Rua, the first carver, felled a tree in the forest, without first placating Tane, the god of the forest. The *Te Tini-o-te-Hakuturi* rebuked Rua and restored the tree to its upright position in the forest. When Rua apologized, another tree was cut down, with Tane's blessing, and a canoe was made from it by the nature spirits. The carved bow and stern were made by spiders, and consequently, Rua incorporated spider webs into his designs.

Webster's New International Dictionary,

Te Pehi face.

Wonders of the Faerie Realm

Ted Andrews
March 2000

For many years I was associated with a nature center. I worked in its animal program and I also served as one of the center's trail guides. I took groups of kids and adults out into nature and taught about its various aspects.

I particularly loved working with the preschoolers because...well, first of all, you don't have to walk very far with them. And second of all, you don't need to get real botanical and technical. I would take them along a wonderful trail and talk about the fairy lore associated with the plants and trees.

One day I was leading a small group of about 15 preschoolers, their teacher and a few of their parents. I came to a spot where there was a natural mound.

Mounds are raised areas in the earth and most traditions taught at one time that communities of fairies and spirits often live within them—hence the common name "fairy mound."

I was standing in front of the group telling them about the fairy mounds. The teacher smiled at me and then spoke to the group of kids, "Well, we don't really believe in fairies and elves, do we?"

The group was silent. They lowered their eyes, not looking at the teacher.

I smiled to myself, thinking, This is interesting…let's take it a little further.

I proceeded to tell a bit more about the fairy mounds, and as I was talking a small boy from the back stepped forward. He put his hands on his hips and looked up at me. Then in a challenging voice, he said, "How do they get in and out of there, then?"

I smiled and said, "Many people think it is through the small openings at the bottoms of the trees nearby."

At that moment a little girl stepped up and said, "They do not. They use this flower and this flower and this one over here." And she proceeded to point out specific flowers.

The girl's mother blushed. The teacher rolled her eyes, and I was jumping up and down inside yelling, "Yes!"

We moved on at that point, but through the rest of our hike, the boy was plastered to my one leg and the girl to the other. Finally, an adult who knew what they had been experiencing.

A little further on we came to a boardwalk that crossed our pond. I led the group across, and as we got to the middle, I paused to talk.

"You know, they used to say that if you tickled the water just right, all of the water fairies would come out, riding on the backs of dragonflies."

I then coaxed everyone down onto the walkway. I even made the teacher and parents do it. Then with the tips of our fingers we tickled the surface of the water for several minutes. When we stood up, there must have been 200 or more dragonflies soaring around us.

It was one of the most wonderful hikes that I ever led at the center. I got some interesting mail from it, but it was truly amazing!

The Faerie Realm

There is still a place where enchantment lives—where streams sing and winds whisper. Where caverns lead to nether realms. Where trees speak and flowers tell tales. Where unicorns dance in the morning dew.

Nothing fires the imagination more than the idea of faeries and elves. And even though our modern world relegates them to the realm of fiction, they touch a chord within us.

Fairies. Elves. Gnomes. Nature spirits. Devas. Unicorns. Dragons. The Realm of Faerie is filled with all of these wonders and more. Skeptics will say that this realm should never be taken literally. They will say that this realm and all of its inhabitants are nothing more than the stuff of fiction. They are a product of the imagination since no scientific data record its presence.

Humans have a tendency to be smug, and many times as people grow older their ability to be open and see the world as the child sees it declines. When this happens the world becomes a place of fear rather than a place of wonder and enchantment.

It is not the purpose of this article to prove the existence of the Faerie Realm or the reality of my own and others' experiences with it. Rarely does the scientific community accept anecdotal evidence. The experiences of others can be a barometer—a map by which others can measure and chart new experiences of wonder.

Every tradition in the world at some point taught that all aspects of Nature have a spirit associated with it. This phenomena of common threads should give us pause. It is a reminder that there is something universal, something wonderful happening around us.

The truth is that most of us have had encounters with the Faerie Realm but did not realize it at the time.

- Have you ever seen movements out of the corner of your eyes that could not be explained? This usually occurs when contact is beginning to open more clearly.
- Do you know that talking to your plants help them to grow? The spirit in the plant responds to you.
- As a child did you have an imaginary friend? Most children's imaginary friends are drawn to the child because of their openness.
- Do you find things disappearing and reappearing around your house frequently? Those of this realm often do this to get our attention.
- Do you dream of strange beasts and places? They can reflect travels into this realm.
- Are your favorite times of the day dawn and dusk? Favorite times of the year the equinoxes and solstices? These are powerful times for Faerie Realm

experiences.

When we experience the Faerie realm Realm, we do so through the five senses. We may see flickering lights around plants or shadowy faces in the trees. We may hear the whispered voices of the pine as a breeze brushes through it, or we may hear music from unexplained sources. A tinkling of bells is a common sound experience.

We may also feel their presence. They stimulate goose bumps. We get a chill or a change of pressure in the air around us. We get the "fly walking through the hair" kind of feeling.

One of the strongest senses by which we experience them is through the sense of smell. Have you ever walked down the street and caught the fragrance of a flower or tree? Most traditions teach that this is a greeting.

Extend a greeting back.

The more you acknowledge the greetings, the stronger they will become around you. I operate on the assumption that most people think I am a little bit strange. (Hard to believe, isn't?) If my neighbors see me talking to a tree, they just usually roll their eyes, and bring their kids inside until I'm gone.

Experiment with the Faerie Realm

On a still day, when there is no breeze, try the following activities:

Sit beside a pond while the water is perfectly still. Hold out a set of wind chimes and tinkle them over the water. Within a minute, bubbles will rise, the water will ripple, as the song of the chimes calls the water spirits to the surface.

Sit beneath a tree, close your eyes and play a flute of some kind for about a minute. If you do not have a flute, whistle one of your favorite childhood tunes. Within 30 to 60 seconds, the leaves will rustle and a breeze will brush over you as you call the air spirits. (It doesn't matter whether you play the flute or whistle well at all.)

Every flower has its fairy. Every tree has its spirit. When we learn to recognize this, we open ourselves to wonderful possibilities. We can uncover some of the secrets of that plant. If nothing else, it will help us in working with the herbal qualities of the plant. And we can use this to our benefit in many areas of our life.

We know that all plants have their own energy, their own spirit. If you are having trouble with aches and pains, go sit under a willow tree for about 10-15 minutes. Just feel the embrace of the tree around you. The aches and pains will disappear.

If we look at it from an herbal aspect, we know that within willow bark is a chemical called salicylate. This is the basis of modern aspirin.

If you have trouble handling strong emotions—especially feelings of guilt—go sit under a pine or evergreen for a bit. Let the spirit of the tree embrace you. I have a wonderful blue spruce in my front yard, and I am often found sitting under it a half hour before my family visits…and several hours afterward. (Bless their hearts.)

Every plant, every aspect of the natural world, has some spirit, some energy associated with it. The fairies and elves are Mother Earth's children. They are her caretakers and they are no further from us than we allow. They hold the key to many of the mysteries of life and nature. They stimulate intuition, creativity, and artistic energies. They hold the secrets to the healing powers of plants, stones, and all of nature.

If we open ourselves to them once more, they will bless our lives many times over. We can open ourselves through simple activities:

❀ Spend time in nature.

❀ Meditate beneath a tree.

❀ Involve yourself in a creative activity. (It doesn't matter whether you are good at it or not, as long as you have fun doing it.)

- Leave an area of your yard to grow free and wild.
- Sing often. The nature spirits gather wherever there is song and music.

As we open to this realm we will soon realize that the fairies and elves have a variety of shapes and forms. They range in size from the tiniest of pixies to great forest devas. They can be larger than a redwood or tinier than a firefly. Their shapes are changeable and they will often use glamour to show themselves only in the way they choose or the way they think you will more likely accept them.

Signs of Faerie Presence

- A sudden, unexplained trembling or whispering of leaves.
- A whirlwind or dust devil.
- The bending of grass blades with no perceptible cause.
- Sudden, unexplained chills and goose flesh when alone in nature.
- Unexplainable losses of time.

There are places and times best for seeking out those of the Faerie Realm. These are called "'Tween Times and Places." They are indistinct. Neither one time or another, neither one place or another. Dawn and dusk for example. They are neither day nor night. They are in-between. Seashores and creek beds are neither part of the land nor part of the water. They are in-between.

Wherever there is an in-between time or place there is a thinning of the veils between worlds and dimensions and it is easier to experience new realms and wonders.

Sometimes in life it is more important to feel than to know. By stirring some of those forgotten embers, by remembering what we felt as a child, were discover the joys and mysteries of the world.

Remember that we can starve as much from a lack of wonder as we can from a lack of food. Nature and all of her spirits and beings keep the wonder in us alive.

May your eyes be always open.

May your hearts overflow.
That which enchants will also protect.
May this you always know.

The Moon People

Lois Allen
June 2000

This is the story of a strange but true happening which I can not explain. There was a full moon and I was lying on my bed with a moonbeam shining brightly into the room. Suddenly, little people began to appear: first, three young people, then three couples, two very near where I lay, and a few older stragglers. In each of the two nearest couples, the young man was holding the hand of a little boy. The woman was holding the hand of a little girl. The third couple, a little farther away, had one child. They had very human expressions of concern about the children. These people seemed very real, the men about three-and-a-half feet tall, and the women much shorter. I looked them over very carefully and they looked solid, as though they were made of a warm, orange sand. Their little figures were just like ours and they had beautiful faces. I don't remember about their clothes.

This little procession started along one side of the bed where I lay, but their feet seemed stuck as though there was glue on them. They would strain and strain for several minutes and then break through and lurch forward a little way, only to be stuck again. The children did not seem to be as stuck as the grown-ups. The men had the most difficult time. I was amazed that these figures were so much like us, with joints in their arms and legs. I wondered whether they could be made out of clay, or wood, or metal, they were so solid.

I studied them for about twenty minutes as they made their slow progress along the side of the bed, and then a right-angle turn around the foot of the bed. The three older persons bringing up the rear seemed in great difficulty, trying to move. Then the young people rounded the far corner of my bed and started up the other side toward where I lay.

All this time I had watched them trying to free their feet from the glue. They would bend forward, and strain and strain, trying to break their feet free. Finally, I had enough of these strange little people. I said in a loud voice, "Beat it! Get out of here!"

The room was dark and silent. I had not realized that this had been happening in a warm, peach-colored atmosphere. The light was gone. The color was gone. My visitors were gone. Perhaps these people were from the moon, or another planet. Maybe they had gone tobogganing on a moon-beam to our planet. Then I realized the glue must have been the gravity pull of the earth. What do you think?

I don't know the answer as to who these people were, but I do know that their presence was a reality.

A Jaunty Moonbeam Man

Lois Allen
July 2000

I have always been affected by the full moon and unable to sleep. My cabin in the Smoky Mountains is surrounded by tall pines, which allow just a little moonlight to come into the room in small patches.

One moonlit night, I opened my bedroom door that leads onto a small porch surrounded by a railing. As I stepped into this area of filtered moonlight, I saw a debonair young man sitting on the corner of the railing. His arms were out to his sides bracing himself, the right arm extended on the far side of the corner, and the left bent closer to his body, but still holding onto the joined rail for a firm support. One leg was crossed over the other with his foot swinging nonchalantly.

He was an extremely tall, thin young man, and he was made of moonlight. His arms and legs were like poles and I found I could see right through them. He had knee joints in his legs and joints in his arms, but he was completely transparent. I had the feeling that he was very much alive and embarking on an exciting evening. There was a jaunty confidence in the way he leaned against my porch railing.

I was so startled that I was unable to move for a few moments. Then, stepping back I slammed the door and bolted it. Later I was furious with myself for not talking to such a strange visitor. I'll never know who or what this young man was, but I do know that he was a very real presence.

The Hidden People of Iceland

Tom R. Kovach
September 2000

Iceland is a very modern country. There is no poverty. It is a country geared toward high technology with literacy standing at 100 percent. But then again, some folks in Iceland still believe in elves, or "Hidden People" as they are referred to.

Sometimes highway engineers will reroute roads because of supposed elf dwellings. And builders of shopping malls take care when they lay electrical cables and other underground installations, so they do not interfere with the suspected homes of elves.

But do Icelanders really believe in the "hidden people"?

Arni Bjornsson, former director of the Ethnological Department of the National Museum, says that according to his investigations and experience, the overwhelming majority of Icelanders do not take the question of hidden people or elves seriously. "However," he says, "quite a lot of them like to play with the thought that there might exist some supernatural beings, although they do not believe it."

Iceland is the most geographically remote of Europe's nations, with a thin population (just over a quarter million people) forged out of fire and ice. Olafur Ragnar Grimsson, the President of Iceland, theorizes that the surfeit of spirit creatures stems from Icelanders' sense of isolation and loneliness. "Icelanders are few in number, so in the old times we doubled our population with tales of elves and fairies," the President said.

But how much of Iceland's belief in elves is tied to impressing the media is something that must be taken into consideration. About 25 years ago the parapsychological institute of Icelandic University made a public opinion poll about many such questions. The result was that around 10 percent believed in the existence of some supernatural beings, another 10 percent categorically denied such possibilities, and around 80 percent neither believed nor denied the possibility of supernatural beings. And these skeptics make up the majority.

Bjornsson said the Icelanders who sincerely believe in various sorts of supernatural beings are very popular with the mass media, who are always looking for something strange and exotic. "Most people are very honest, these believers, and they are certainly not lying deliberately," said Bjornsson. "It would therefore be almost impolite to question their truthfulness. This is one of the reasons so many people are skeptical...although they do not believe themselves."

Bjornsson adds that there is no doubt that a certain connection with Icelandic tolerance in religious matters plays into the belief in the supernatural. "Elsewhere most people are ashamed to admit a belief in the supernatural. In Iceland people are not ashamed—on the contrary, some of them are rather proud of their 'abilities.'"

But do elves really interfere with the building of roads?

"The question about contractors and road builders, in regards to the elves, needs a special explanation," said Bjornsson.

"Iceland is 103,000 square kilometers large," he said, "and most of its settlements are not very big. Until about 200 years ago there were no towns in this country. There were practically no roads in the country until about 100 years ago. You had to travel on your own feet or on horseback. When we began to build roads for wagons and cars in the beginning of the 20th century, there were no bulldozers. The narrow roads had to go around hills and cliffs."

Then in the second half of the twentieth century, Iceland got modern equipment. "The engineers naturally wanted to build the roads as straight as possible," said Bjornsson. "They wanted to demolish the old hills and cliffs. And this was made a rule. However, there are some examples that certain people protested. Some for environmental reasons, others because they maintained that a certain cliff or hill was inhabited by hidden people (the *huldufolk*)."

Unfortunately, these protests were usually ignored. "But there were a few examples when contractors made some compromises with the people," Bjornsson said.

"This was especially true if it was rather easy to move the road a little. Most often such a compromise was not made because of the hidden people as such, but because the contractors did not want to hurt the feelings of the people involved unnecessarily, and possibly make themselves unpopular."

But in a land overrun with gnomes, trolls, fairies, elves, and *huldufolk*, it becomes easier to see why so many Icelanders feel they are sharing their little island with other beings.

Bjornsson sums it up: "Our country seems custom-designed for superstition. Such an extreme landscape inspires visions of the supernatural. The everyday reality surrounding Icelanders would be called hallucinations or nightmares anywhere else—hot-water geysers, molten rock, terrible earthquakes, and the cold sea raging all around. No wonder we have odd tales!"

Pu'ukohola Heiau, Temple of the Whales.

Temple of the Whales

Richard D. Seifried
October 2001

The date was July 1965. I was standing in my dormitory room in the Twin Towers of the University of Hawaii. My roommate was telling me about events that had happened on the Big Island, Hawaii.

I couldn't have picked a more modern, sanitized environment. The new dormitory buildings reflected modern American architecture; nothing suggesting native Hawaiian influence could be discerned.

Yet, my roommate, a tall, slender gentleman who had been born and raised in Tennessee, related events that he obviously believed to be true but could not explain. His stories were not unlike countless other tales recorded in Hawaii's Polynesian history.

I don't remember my friend's name. He was married to a Hawaiian lady and lived somewhere along the Kona Coast, probably south of Kailua. That's coffee country, and my roommate managed his wife's small coffee plantation. Suddenly, it seemed, he felt compelled to relate to me his tales, trusting that I, living in American Samoa, would understand and not laugh.

The Tennesseean's Tales

The first story was typical of Hawaiian lore. An acquaintance, a Hawaiian lady, had been riding in a taxi near where she lived on the Big Island. The woman's husband sat in the front seat beside the Hawaiian driver. She and her daughter shared the back part of the vehicle. Suddenly a very beautiful young lady appeared next to her.

The stranger was obviously Hawaiian, possessing long, black hair and delicate, Polynesian features.

They immediately knew who she was. The wonderful apparition was Pele-'aihonus, "Pele who eats the land," the fire goddess who lives inside Kilauea crater, located on the lower southern slopes of the 13,796-foot-high volcano, Mauna Kea.

Finally she spoke. Pele told her Hawaiian companions that three days hence, Mauna Kea would once more erupt and that lava would flow thorough a small Hawaiian village. The people must leave or they would die.

According to my university friend, the eruption occurred just as Pele had predicted. In my own mind I wondered if his story was merely a legend, nothing more. Sensing my skepticism he went on to tell me the other story, how when the lava had cooled, his wife had taken him to an old Hawaiian cemetery.

Fresh lava had covered the burial place. But, in one small spot, where a Hawaiian king had been buried, the lava had separated, swept around both sides of the grave and rejoined below. My friend had found himself looking down 15 feet or so, where the king's gravestone stood, unharmed.

There was no reason to disbelieve him. Why would he lie?

Nothing Out of the Ordinary

Manoa Falls, Oahu

I have been to Hawaii several times. My son and his family reside there. But, to my past disappointment, nothing "unusual" ever happened to me.

My visits took me to places like isolated Manoa Falls, deep in the rain forest, above the university. Like countless other visitors, I have stood on the edge of the Pali on Oahu, where King Kamehameha I's army drove hundreds of his enemies over the cliffs in the battle that won him the island of Oahu. With a friend I stood on the enchanting cliffs of Makapuu Point, watching the soundings and cavorting of the mighty humpback whales.

On the Big Island, Hawaii, walking alone, I have photographed some of the hundreds of splendid pictographs found along a path crossing a barren lava bed. I have strolled in parks where, sometimes at night, the Coast Walkers, the giant ghosts of Hawaiian warriors, are sometimes seen moving silently in a long line, torches held high above their ethereal heads. But nothing unusual had ever assailed my senses.

In March 2001, I once again went with my son and his family to the Kona Coast. One evening we enjoyed a program given by a Hawaiian couple. They sang and told stories, mostly bits and pieces of rather inaccurate island history.

Don't Take the Rocks

The entertainers gave us a warning. "Don't take any lava rocks back to the mainland. If you do, sooner or later you will have bad luck and will believe that Pele is angry and you must return the stolen rocks.

"That isn't true," they concluded. Actually, some enterprising mainlander made up the story, and now it is widely believed. The entertainer went on to say, "Everyone has bad luck." He laughed at his remark. "Don't take any rocks! Our post offices have boxes and boxes of returned rocks and they don't know what to do with them." We all joined in with his laughter.

Two days later, March 28, we drove up the coast to a location supervised by the National Park Service. It is called Pu'ukohola Heiau National Historic Site.

There are three *heiau* (temples) on the NPS property. One, Hale o Kapuni Heiau, lies submerged, just offshore, covered with silt. That *heiau* is dedicated to the shark god. Up from the shore stand the remains of Mailekini Heiau. Apparently the purpose for its construction has been lost, because visitors are told that the round stone structured *heiau* may have been a war, or perhaps, an agricultural temple.

Greatest of all and most recently built towers the magnificent Pu'ukohola Heiau, the temple on the Hill of the Whales.

The Whale Temple

By 1790, Kamehameha I had conquered the islands of Maui, Lanai, and Molokai, but he was unable to gain control of the Big Island, Hawaii. According to Hawaiian history, the great prophet Kapoukahi sent word that if Kamehameha built a great temple atop Pu'ukohola, "Hill of the Whales," at Kawaihae, and dedicated the edifice to his family war god, Ku, Kamehameha would become ruler of all of the Hawaiian Islands.

Since such structures had to be built of wave-smoothed lava rocks, the great king ordered thousands of men to camp out along a coastal trail. The rocks were passed from the seaside valley of Pololu, from one warrior to another, for over 20 miles. The project took over a year to complete.

Today, Pu'ukohola Heiau stands majestically overlooking the sea. The buildings and idols that once adorned the interior are gone, but three long,

Pali Cliff, where Kamehameha I's warriors drive the opposing army over the edge.

terraced steps still lead upward to the ceremonial courtyard. The structure measures 224 by 100 feet and is enclosed on all sides, except the one facing the Pacific, by magnificent stone walls that stand between 16 and 20 feet high. To see inside, one must use an outrigger canoe and paddle offshore for a short distance.

Visit to the Temple

We left the visitor center and walked down the path toward the temple on the Hill of the Whales. The name was significant to us because we had observed several humpback whales spouting, cavorting, and splashing their tails, just a quarter of a mile or so offshore on our way to the park.

My son's wife and children walked a short distance ahead of us. We moved slowly downward, across the near-barren hillside to a point just below the temple's imposing structure. The round, stone walls towered above us, just a few yards away. Deeply impressed, we read the sign positioned where an upward leading trail left our paved pathway. It read:

Kapu
This Heiau (Temple) is
sacred to Hawaiians please
respect their beliefs
GO NO FARTHER

Silence at the Temple

My son and I stopped and studied the dirt pathway angling upward toward the temple. Magnificent round stone walls loomed high above us, appearing to rise high into the deep blue, tropical sky. Path, hillside, and temple reflected a somber hue that reminded me of Anasazi ruins in the American Southwest. No wind blew. I heard no birds, and I saw no insect, tree, or flower.

My mind, awed at what I beheld, wondered what the temple looked like within the walls. Were there still holy images, stone posts, or wooden ruins of sacred altars? I wondered if unthinking visitors ignored the sign and climbed the barren path. Did Hawaiians ignore the sign and violate the holy temple with their presence? I thought not. Hawaiians wouldn't trespass on sacred land. Mainlanders would; a few.

We studied the temple for some time. I took some pictures.

There She Blows!

My son was below me, about 30 feet away, on the paved trail, still gazing upward. His little boy stood perhaps 20 feet below him. We stood in a sort of line, perpendicular to the temple walls. The girls had gone on toward the sea. Turning, I gazed out over the sparkling sea and the thought passed through my mind, "I wonder if I can see the whales from here?"

SHISSSSSSHHHH! A terrible, powerful sound caused me to turn back toward the temple on the Hill of the Whales.

Out of the extreme top, a bit to the left of the right wall, where the main altar had been, a tremendous surge of air swept up from the hidden floor of the *heiau*. At first, the whirling wind was no more than 20 feet across. The force, a tremendous funnel of air, roared down the slope, moving directly toward us. As it did, stone chips, some half an inch in diameter, became airborne. Unlike the devil-dusters of the central states, the wind remained almost invisible, except for the stones and bits of dust. By the time it reached our path, the diameter had spread to perhaps 40 feet.

The sign.

The spirit wind took mere seconds—at most four or five—to reach our trail. We had time only to prepare ourselves before it struck us.

A Near Thing

If I hadn't been braced against its onslaught, I would have tumbled off the path and fallen downhill, undoubtedly becoming injured. As it was, the wind pushed me all the way off the path and a few feet beyond. I am a large man, over six feet and weighing 185 pounds. My son, probably 50 pounds heavier than I, was also struck with such violence that he, too, braced against the onslaught, was pushed off the paved walkway.

As soon as the force struck us, it dissipated, becoming a short-lived downhill breeze.

Rock fragments had assailed my arms and legs, dealing me painful blows. At first I thought that my legs were bleeding. No hard particles had struck my glasses. In fact, my grandson, who had been just at the edge of the wind, and my son and I received not a single fragment of dust in our unprotected eyes. Dirt covered our faces and coated our hair but we were, except for my stinging legs, virtually unharmed.

Instantly I thought back over what might have triggered the supernatural rush of energy. I remembered my last thought, "I wonder if I can see the whales from here?" Turning to my son I told him what I had mentally asked myself. He responded, "Why, that is exactly what I was thinking, too."

A bit later, my pragmatic scientist son said something like, "I never believed in things like that but I guess I have to, now." He walked on down the pathway.

Rebuking the Spirit

I continued gazing up at the somber, silent, stone walls. Learning long ago not to be intimidated by the unknown, I realized that if whatever it was had been able to read my thoughts about the whales, then that same spirit could also read what else I would think.

Silently I thought the following, addressing the unknown force of Pu'ukoholo Heiau. "You should be more discerning as to whom and why you attack with such power. I meant you no harm. I was not about to climb the forbidden trail or desecrate your sacred temple space. I meant you no harm and had nothing but respect for your temple. Yet, you hurt me, tried to harm me, expressed your anger over the intrusion of my innocent thinking about the whales."

I thought more words, but I cannot remember them. My reaction was indignation and a little anger. Perhaps the spirit was having fun but I was offended.

No response came from the stone *heiau*. I saw and felt only an unemotional recognition emanating from the walled temple. No anger in response to my scolding. No humor. Only something hovering above me, something that dwelled within the great stone Hawaiian shrine.

The Great Gremlin Caper

Dave Stern
December 2001

Boris Artzybasheff, 1942

Numerous "Zoners" (*Twilight Zone* fans) and others may remember a 1963 *Twilight Zone* episode starring William Shatner. The future captain of the *Enterprise* plays a thoroughly terrified airline passenger who alone observes an ugly, gnarled critter land on the wing and tamper with the engine, which is running at nearly full throttle. John Lithgow reprised the role in *Twilight Zone: The Movie.* Richard Matheson, the author of the story upon which this show is based, drew inspiration from the World War II activities of certain strange, miniature creatures. Crafty Steven Spielberg used his own nightmare vision of them in his feature length movie, *Gremlins.*

Little People

During WW II, the toxic mental climate of fear, terror, and the mindset to kill or be killed rippled through the atmosphere. The intangible fabric of the ether was severely affected by such tremendous negativity, thus upsetting nature's reasonably tranquil balance. The long-haunted United Kingdom and Europe possessed numerous traditions of little people that lent support to their modern reappearance between the World Wars.

Nearly every culture possesses myths and legends concerning miniature biped creatures that harass, vex, interact, and interfere with man's life. They describe numerous diminutive creatures with a variety of names that reach far into man's ancient history. The most popular term used in children's books is "fairy."

This term comes from antiquity, and is possibly derived from the Persian word *peri*, later rearranged in Old French as *faerie, fae,* or *faierie*. Near Eastern cultures also record a similar category of little people in the *djinn*, or *jinnee*, eventually corrupted into the English term "genie." The word "gnome" also represented a wise little person, or "one who knows things."

The European continent was also haunted by the goblin, imp, fay, nymph, puck, pixie, sylph, troll, and gnome; Germany had kobolds, gnome-like creatures, said to live in mines, while authenticated reports speak of Bean-sidhe, or Banshee, a woman-fairy. The Hawaiian natives spoke reverently of the little *menehunes.*

Ireland has its leprechauns (also called Good People), supposedly living within or under prehistoric earthworks called tumuli, raths, forts, or duns. Also in Ireland, the strange term *Na Fir Glorm* referred to a breed of little blue men. Greek and Roman legends describe maidens called dryads living in trees, while brownies were little creatures that loved old farmhouses. Near Ulster, Ireland, there were even little spirits called *geancanach* or sprites. The ancient Celts had their tales of miniature people who mysteriously went about their earth business. For lack of a better idea, some believed that fairies were God's fallen angels.

Explanations

In the last 100 years, at least two different explanations have been offered concerning the little-people phenomenon. Hilarian, the author of *Dark Robes, Dark Brothers* (Marcus Books, Toronto, 1981) offers a chilling statement about these miniature, human-looking creatures. In order to interact and interfere with us on the physical plane, the Dark Brothers manipulate

The Royal Air Force's famous WW II "Battle of Britain" Supermarine Spitfire fighter that beat the German Luftwaffe. Gremlins went after anything that sported wings, yet German airman were puzzled when Allied Intelligence specialists interrogated them about Gremlin activity. The Germans suffered the usual machinery breakdowns, but not Gremlin problems. This lends credence to the *Dark Brothers* theory that only Allied airmen were tormented.

and mold energy to create automaton or robot entities at the etheric level. They are considered quite real and have the specific mission of interacting with humanity.

The other explanation describes such activity as being individual psychokinesis (PK), human psychic energy stimulated by powerful emotions that in turn are transmitted through the psychic eye or pineal gland. This human bioelectrical energy can heavily interact with machinery, causing various negative and troublesome reactions, especially where airplanes are concerned.

In recent times, a 20th-century counterpart to the ancient legends of little people suddenly reappeared out of nowhere while humanity was engaged in two World Wars. The uncanny aspect of their visitations is that they seemed specifically focused on interacting with airmen and their flying machines.

The phenomenon did generate lighthearted moments among the Allied forces, thus momentarily relieving the nightmare severity of combat. The violence of WW II is peppered with accounts of many extraordinary physical and occult events that remain unsolved to this day, although the strange gremlin capers levied against the Royal Air Force and the USAAF became public domain in 1942. According to the British, the first modern recorded appearance of these little people dates back to the 1920s.

The Gremlins Manifest

The modern legend began when they supposedly popped out of a bottle of beer being consumed by a Fleet Air Arm pilot in 1923. This particular naval pilot max-grossed his weight on beer one evening prior to a scheduled A.M. flight. Next morning, the pilot strapped himself into a marginal reconnaissance aeroplane that suffered perpetual engine troubles. Once airborne, he was catapult-launched from his ship, the engine stopped dead, and said aeroplane crashed into the sea.

Upon being recovered, the wet, cold, and now sober pilot sputtered something about little people jumping out of a beer bottle and tormenting him all night; it was they who entered the plane's engine and raised hell with it while others attacked his controls, thus causing the crash.

In a move that was anything but charitable, these strange little beings suddenly appeared at an overseas RAF aerodrome in 1925. A few RAF sergeant pilots stationed there began encountering them and colloquially tagged their annoying interferences as "gremlin action." This term was drawn from the old English term *greme*, which literally means to vex and annoy. The term stuck shortly after the critters attacked. The little bipeds quickly moved to other RAF aerodromes and immediately caused problems with squadron aircraft.

To be fair about the matter, an alternate legend offers us the tale of troubled groundlings, those maintenance and operations people working in the

British radio and electronics industry. They supposedly encountered unusual repetitious radio and radar malfunctions and blamed this trouble on "little men" who entered the sets and caused havoc.

Gremlins were the subject of countless cartoons and children's books. This specimen was published in 1943 by E. P. Dutton.

As the air war gained momentum, so too did the appearance of what were variously called pixies, silversnicks, aerial pixies, gnome (pronounced "genomey"), pixilators, little people, spandules, widgets, the bat-eared *Duticulatus prangiferos*, gremlins, and little green men.

The Americans contributed Yehudi (after a famous but unrelated violinist who was totally innocent of anything concerning gremlins), Butch Yehudi (an American Eagle Squadron pilot's term for the leader of little biped-entities that "fiddled around" with his aircraft), and last but not least, the stateside strato-gremlins.

The gremlins had girlfriends and wives known as finellas or fifinellas, who took great interest in their men's work. The miniature babes (who also tormented the airmen) were nicknamed widgets. It was the widgets who constantly asked their brethren, "Do you believe in airmen?"

Meanwhile, airmen quickly respected these creatures because they demanded to be called "they," "them," "it," or "she"; actually, gremlins preferred being called "them," since it generated feelings of intangible power. The British learned not to laugh at them, and soon intuited their mission of tormenting airmen and interrupting their flying activities during aerial combat.

Their behavior ranged from an odd sense of skewed humor to prank and panic specialists that, while playful on the one hand, seemed intent on "doing in" a pilot or aircrew (according to the British), especially the troublesome spandules. The British chaps eventually sorted them out by color: The good ones wore blue or red, while the bad dudes wore green or yellow. However, the best of the lot seemed to be the gremlins wearing green waistcoats.

American airmen were probably relieved that a Grumman Gremlin (it has an agreeable ring that also fits one other company) fighter or floatplane was never built, lest it suffer no end of insoluble pixie problems during prototype testing. But only the mystically inclined "Mister Mac" (James Smith McDonnell), founder of McDonnell Aircraft Corporation in St. Louis, could and did get away with identifying his aircraft by supernatural terms right out of June G. Bletzer's *Encyclopedic Psychic Dictionary.*

"Mr. Mac" might have named his diminutive late-1940s parasite fighter the XF-85 Gremlin instead of Goblin, and it wouldn't have made any difference. Indeed, the little shrieking, turbine-powered "strap-on Goblin" looked like a sinister winged troublemaker, and a surviving example resides at the Air Force Museum in Dayton Ohio. Mr. Mac's other famous fighters were called the Banshee, Demon, Voodoo, Phantom I, and the "Phabulous" Phantom II.

It was the sharp "Mark-Ones" (eyes) of British and American volunteers in the Eagle Squadrons that sized up their tormenters and reported mind-bending descriptions to their unbelieving brethren. These vexatious critters ranged in height from five inches to approximately one foot and swapped claws for suction pads during their high-altitude torments.

Gremlins were observed sporting aerodynamically streamlined heads and possessed high intellect and sharp telepathic abilities: They easily anticipated and outmaneuvered even the quickest-reacting pilots during combat. Their apparel included designer-style tights, stocking caps with tassels, and pointed, elfin-like footwear. Their double-breasted frock coats were described as red or green with optional neck-ruffles, and there were the odd, flat-topped tricorn hats with a feather, plus the occasional "natty" gremlin wearing spiffy white spats.

Aircrew stand by as a Naval Air Cadet boards an NAA SNJ-6 trainer in preparation for a training flight in Pensacola, Florida near the war's end. Gremlins disliked pilots who exhibited a lack of finesse in handling their aircraft, and consequently, a pilot's negative attitude drew extra attention from the gremlins.

RAF personnel complained about the gremlins causing engines that ran fine the night before to refuse to start the next morning. Next, the petrol tanks suddenly began dribbling fuel all over the underwings and fuselage, while previously tight hydraulic brakes leaked like a sieve and tires quickly sagged from a mysterious loss of air.

The gremlins' capers slowly escalated when squadron aircraft were equipped with retractable landing gear, turbochargers, liquid cooling systems, and newer radios—accessories that offered more items to disrupt. RAF maintenance officers, and especially the airframe and engine fitters, were astounded that numerous aircraft, having just been fully repaired and returned to service (RTS), severely deteriorated overnight and were promptly regrounded the next morning.

Gremlin Types

The RAF chaps eventually identified the various gremlins and their particular interference specialty. There were Petrol Boozers with huge eyes and a large retractable vacuum nose that came in two distinct species: one strictly addicted to 75- octane gas, while the other demanded nothing less than 100-octane fuel. While the RAF's fuel bowsers filled an airplane's tanks on the ground, the Petrol Boozers quickly drained them in flight, leaving barely enough gasoline for one landing (no missed approaches or go-arounds) and a brief taxi. The Brits also identified the Rubber-Nibbler, who attacked tires, stripped electrical wire of its insulation, and caused circuit breakers to pop in flight.

The cynical Tropical Gremlin jammed sand into the air filters of RAF desert-based fighters and bombers, while the Duty Gremlin lowered runways, causing bomber and fighter pilots to bounce during messy three-point landings. Still others moved trees up and into the path of aircraft on final approach, while the odd Hangar-Owl, living in the rafters, was responsible for "hangar-queens," logging more ground time than flight hours.

Little is mentioned of the Officer's Mess Gremlin, but the Accountancy Gremlin's obnoxious speciality was erasing log-book entries and service forms. They were also blamed for committing depredations against new aircraft designs on the drawing-boards, thus causing some prototypes to perform so badly that they were never mass produced. The RAF's Coastal Command suffered from Sharp or Sword-nosed Gremlins, who punched holes and slashed away at the fabric on the aircraft's control surfaces. They loved to punch holes in float-plane pontoons, which, upon landing, filled with water, causing the aircraft to list.

The frustrating little bipeds made aircraft fitters look especially bad by attacking Flying Boat hulls and causing numerous leaks. Another specialist was the spry little non-flying Spade-nosed Gremlin, who dug holes in airfield runways. He caused aircraft to drop into the hole, flipping the plane nose-down, thus pranging skin, nose bubbles, formers, and propellers.

Meanwhile, the Hairy-legged Gremlin of Gibraltar possessed a triangular hole in its abdomen. The wind shrilly whistled through it, leading a pilot to mistakenly believe he was flying faster than the airspeed indicator was

The diminutive McDonnell XF-85 Goblin "strap-on" escort or parasite fighter hung from a trapeze in the bomb bay of a large bomber. The mystical minded James McDonnell, who founded McDonnell Aircraft in St. Louis, Missouri, named his fighters after mythical and sinister characters, and also donated funds to paranormal research groups. Had it been named the Gremlin, the plane would still be the same little shrieking rip-snorter.

reading and causing the pilot to stall his plane and crash.

Pigeon Antidote

The RAF discovered that the gremlin's arch enemy was the humble pigeon. According to an American reporter stationed in London, RAF reconnaissance planes carried messenger pigeons during their missions.

Only the bravest gremlins dared to muck around with the pilot or his aircraft when pigeons were aboard. Pilots also discovered that wearing certain talismans seemingly negated their nefarious behavior. Carrying the traditional American rabbit's foot, clover leaf, lucky coin, a special scarf, and the "gremlin-cradle" (an empty beer bottle), plus other talismans, forced gremlins to lose their nerve and leave a particular aircraft and pilot alone.

But, during combat, airmen were driven to the brink of despair and their quick reactions pushed to the finite limits of human endurance. During aerial combat over Dieppe, Squadron Leader Gus Daymond's Eagle Squadron Spitfire was severely messed with by a gaggle of little bipeds led by the "Butch Gremlin." Having shot down one German FW-190 fighter and pursuing another, he suddenly noticed that gremlins had ganged up on his controls, causing him to misfire, allowing the FW to escape.

Annoying Behavior

During critical moments, the gremlins jabbed British or American pilots in the back where they couldn't scratch, or danced on the Spitfire's gun sight reflector. Some gremlins rode the prop blades as they spun around, while others tinkered with carburetor settings, or sat atop the control sticks, spinning madly about to disorient the pilot.

Fifinellas patiently waited until the instant before a pilot fired his guns at an opponent, then simply reached out and tickled him under the chin to throw off his aim. Other gremlins and fifinellas chattered madly as they danced atop the wings and fuselage, while some flipped the wingtips up and down for extra aggravation. The pilots of Number 71 Eagle Squadron dogfighting the Germans over Dieppe were plagued by holes that suddenly appeared in their fuel tanks, while a Spitfire suffered the rare jammed throttle, forcing the pilot to bail out. Even the night fliers developed jangled nerves when they heard dozens of gremlins madly chattering while dancing on their wings and control surfaces; yet the pilots didn't mind the critters swiping and eating the pilot's issue of carrots for sharpening their night sight.

U.S. Pilots No Exception

The U.S. Army Air Forces fared no better with gremlins than the British. They quickly ganged up on bomber crews, and they loved to knock the sights of the nose machine gun out of line. The complex systems of the B-17s and B-24s were attacked, while the light and medium bombers had their nose-bubble edges chipped away by the gremlins.

The U.S. Army Air Force leaned heavily on Boeing Company to speed up the test program of this prototype B-29 Superfortress bomber. The highly advanced and complex B-29 suffered endless gremlin problems during a rushed test-flight program, but later bombed Japan with incendiaries and the first atomic bombs.

This nasty work generated ice-cold drafts and caused a nerve-jangling whistle of air that whipped through the cracks. Many a bomber navigator suffered a poke in the ribs or a jab in the armpit while taking a crucial reading with his sextant. There were also strange reports about tail gunners who allowed the little bipeds to join them in their cramped combat offices, mostly for the extra warmth and companionship.

Gremlins loved to attack aircraft instrument panels and make the artificial horizon tilt back and forth, while others caused the gyroscopic compass to spin around madly like a top. Even transport pilots became nervous when dozens of pixies danced about the slipstream flowing over their wings. The U.S. Bomber Command's operations people also found themselves plagued by white-collar gremlins who rifled their secret classified files. This groundling specimen tormented everybody by mixing up the minutely prepared mission maps and trashing any semblance of administrative order.

Meanwhile, the gremlins clung to movable control surfaces that generated aileron flutter, while others bit minute holes in the rubber de-icer boots, thus preventing them from working during missions.

The older spandule gremlins never operated below 10,000 feet and were responsible for icing up many aircraft and wings. Pilots swore they never intended to cause fatal accidents, but the gremlins were blamed for moving cloud formations and messing around with the atmospheric pressure that affected certain instruments. Gunners complained about their machine gun barrels inexplicably plugging up, because the little silversnicks with their long bodies and faces slid down the barrels and deflected the shells or caused the triggers to stick.

The Army Air Force also reported that Training Command's aircraft were serving a dual purpose: teaching pilots to fly and giving ankle-biter widgets OJT (on-the-job training) at the expense of the American taxpayer. They cut their teeth on control cables, while others either gnawed on electrical wire insulation or pulled on them until something gave. Other trainee widgets poked and probed for airframe or hydraulic system weakness and ways to interfere with the aircraft's numerous accessories. While the airplane's operating systems were under attack, other gremlins sat on the pilot's shoulders during training flights and made rude noises in their ears.

Further Interference

They perfectly emulated the sounds of a sputtering engine or the thumping of a piston about to seize. When airborne, the gremlins mercilessly tormented the lackadaisical and ham-fisted pilots, simply because they didn't like the way they handled their aircraft. Marginal pilots were often told "you're flying upside down, you fathead"; so the pilot, while actually flying right-side up, immediately flipped the plane over and continued flying inverted.

When the gremlin phenomena was reported in stateside newspapers and magazines, it impressed the civilian population and a New York composer named Raymond Scott. He took one musical score from his Ballet Theatre production *Quintette* and rewrote it to describe Fifinella, "the lily of the airfield."

Although the most intense gremlin activity occurred during the war, they were still the scapegoats for aircraft equipment failures and glitches in the postwar era. Were gremlins strictly a phenomena of WW II? In 1950, Alaska's *49th Star* newspaper, with temerity, republished a short blurb originally published in Nome's *Mukluk Telegraph.* It asked that Eskimos who were constantly observing little men "who aren't there" running about the tundra to contact the *Telegraph.* The paper would then transmit the information to "stateside" scientists who had requested reports on the phenomenon—they believed that the little people might exist!

Through the years, numerous gremlins were blamed for aircraft malfunctions and crashes. In the late 1980s when Delta Airlines and others suffered a rash of flying "incidents," Delta's spokesman, Jim Ewing, got it right when he succinctly stated, "The gremlins are attacking."

With crossed fingers, we now enter the new millennium by establishing a permanent International Space Station in low-earth orbit—but hopefully without the help of hitchhiking cockroaches, let alone any exo-atmospheric or space gremlins.

The Boeing B-17 Flying Fortress, backbone of our WW II bombing campaign, was plagued by gremlins when flying missions over Europe and back home over Puget Sound, Washington. Each bomber was four times as complex as a single-engined fighter, and during flight tests high over Seattle, was visited by little strato-gremlins, who tore through the bomber's complex systems.

The Puget Sound Strato-Gremlins

Dave Stern
December 2001

As World War II raged in Europe and Asia, women and men on the home front worked furiously around the clock to provide the Allies with machines of war. Aircraft firms turned out thousands of fighters, bombers, transports, trainers, and gliders daily. One in particular, the Boeing Company, attracted the attention of *Life* magazine readers back in 1942 with an extraordinary discovery. When the gremlin phenomena was reported in newspapers and magazines throughout America, Boeing test pilots and crews discovered to their consternation that it was not merely an overseas phenomenon.

Boeing pilots worked furiously to flight-test the B-17 Flying Fortress bombers that were constantly being towed across old Highway 99, bordering the Seattle plant. Each day found test crews manning B-17s and flying around beautiful Puget Sound to thoroughly test each aircraft and write up any squawks when systems became inoperative.

A Boeing Company employee informed readers of *Life* that company test pilots were plagued by a breed of miniature bipeds that they nicknamed "strato-gremlins." The test pilots soon realized that these Yankee gremlins possessed an operational altitude of 35,000-plus feet, and because of this trait, they were double the size of the overseas gremlins. The high-altitude gremlins also sported very large noses that greatly resembled the oxygen system's breather-bag. They were described as having blue-tinged fur and much larger ears than the standard-issue gremlin. Although somewhat docile, they liked to poke pilots in the gut once they reached 35,000 feet, although they sometimes accompanied the crews back to *terra firma* while constantly making snapping noises in the aircrew's ears.

During test flights, the little critters minutely examined the B-17's oil system feed lines and drank the oil out of the tanks, causing alarming drops in engine oil pressure. It was they who were blamed for messing with the radio antennas, thus causing static and garbled messages transmitted and received between the crew and company headquarters. They loved to fool around with the propeller and governor controls, and constantly knocked the four engines' RPMs out of sync. Their breath was said to congeal the oil, and when the little widgets entered the lines with soda straws, they blew bubbles that foamed the critical lubricant at high altitudes.

They sat in the cockpit, and while staring out the front windshields, their breath fogged them up, causing Boeing engineers to redesign the armored windshields and cure the fog problem. Many systems were modified after the strato-gremlins were through messing with them, including erratic ignition systems, because they warmed their fingers on the hot spark plugs. They quickly transferred their attentions to the large and complex Boeing B-29 Superfortress bombers also being flight tested. Eventually, the strato-gremlins "lost altitude," gave up their work aboard Boeing's bombers, and transferred themselves into the company Strato Testing Chamber. The retired strato-gremlins are credited with helping to develop stratospheric flight and aiding the successful line of bombers and transport aircraft since then.

A British Poem on Gremlins

Say, you've gotta beware when you're up in the air
And sailing serenely along.
'Cos I often appear with a horrible leer
And make you do everything wrong.
I run up the wing, you can hear a sharp "ting"
As I pull at the wires in the plane,
Then I sit on the prop and the kite starts to hop,
It drives all the pilots insane.
When you're trying to think, with a devilish wink
I proceed to bite lumps off the rudder.
You go down in a spin and I laugh and I grin,
It's enough to make anyone shudder.
So you've gotta beware when you're up in the air,
You might see me appear on the spanner.
I'm a wicked old ____; I know it as well,
I'm a Gremlin, a ___ old sinner!

All photos in this article by Sgt. John Greany, USAAF

The Land-Sea Rescue Team was supplied by another C-47 Gooney Bird like the crashed plane. During one drop near the base camp, boxes popped open in midair, bombing the camp with whole loaves of fresh baked bread provided by Elmendorf Field's bakery.

The Mysterious Mount Deception Wreck

Dave Stern
December 2001

On September 18, 1944, a completely airworthy Air Training Command C-47 flown by a competent aircrew departed Elmendorf AFB with 19 passengers on a routine flight to Ladd Field, Fairbanks. During clear but turbulent weather and a visible full moon, the Gooney Bird failed to

A snow jeep and supply train head for Mount Deception, to locate the wreckage of a USAAF Douglas C-47 transport that collided with the mountain in 1944. It took the Land-Sea Rescue Team 53 days by ground to reach the wreckage site from Anchorage, Alaska.

report to several ground stations and never reached Ladd Field. Both military and civil bush pilots conducted an air search, but it was a B-24 Liberator out of Elmendorf Field that photographed the wreck as it flew near Mt. McKinley.

The wreck's location presented investigators with some very puzzling aspects. The Gooney Bird last reported passing Talkeetna at 9,000 feet, yet it was found to have collided with Mount Deception, next to Mount McKinley, at approximately 19,000 feet. The C-47 was also 60 miles to the left and five miles northwest of the established Anchorage-Fairbanks Airway track that it was supposed to fly along.

Land-Sea troops clearing snow from around the fuselage in an attempt to locate just one human body or pieces thereof. The twisted and split wide open fuselage and several windows show up in this view.

The C-47 slammed at cruise speed smack into the side of Mount Deception. The instant stoppage of a large, multi-ton transport literally split the fuselage open as it telescoped into a mass of twisted aluminum sharp enough to slice and dice human flesh into unrecognizable bits.

Rescue Unit Finally Arrives

A ground-traveling Land Sea Rescue unit was dispatched and reached the wreckage site 53 days later. Provisions were parachuted from overflying transports out of Elmendorf Field. The C-47 was discovered lying on a snow avalanche initiated when it tumbled down the mountain and was partly buried by eight feet of fresh snow. When closely examined, the transport was found to be a total mass of pancaked metal, horribly smashed and twisted except for a portion of the vertical fin.

It was ascertained that the left wing initially hit the mountain, approximately 1,500 feet above its final resting spot, while the port engine and propeller literally imbedded itself into the mountain's blue-green ice near the top of the peak. The plane burst open as it folded into itself, then tumbled down a 50-degree slope that twisted the fuselage in two as the ceiling and floor were flattened together. The violent collision ripped the wings in separate sections, while the cockpit section was twisted from the fuselage—it was actually discovered facing backward from the direction of the impact.

No Trace of Human Remains

The instrument panel was totally trashed, yet a gyro horizon ripped from the panel was found intact several feet away, its glass face unbroken. The plane carried a full load of fuel, but there was no sign of an explosion, nor was any part of the wreck burned. No baggage was found, except for several playing cards, but the unfastened seat belts indicated that the final moments of impact were quite unexpected. The rescue team, headed by Bradford Washburn, found the pilot's B-4 bag outside the cabin. In it was an unbroken bottle of whiskey wrapped in cotton shorts. No bodies nor traces of flesh, blood, hair, or body pieces were found in, around, or under the fuselage, even though the men took turns digging!

Four men climbed to the peak of the mountain in order to lower themselves 220 feet down the face just to reach the engine. The engine and prop were rammed two feet into solid ice on a 53-degree slope. They found aluminum scrap metal and an oxygen bottle, but no signs of human bodies or parts that would have been thrown forward during the instant stoppage. Despite the lack of blood, flesh, or hair, it was conjectured that perhaps the bodies and their baggage had tumbled into a deep crevasse below the aircraft, even though the wreckage site had been excavated and a nearby crevasse examined.

This photo displays the C-47's extreme rear fuselage with its still intact tail wheel. The 1,500- foot tumble down the steep slope of Mt. Deception tore the aircraft into nearly unrecognizable aluminum scrap after the initial impact split open and telescoped the fuselage. The man in the background is wielding an axe to separate the twisted metal and search for bodies or parts.

Whether it be gremlins and or other forces that acted upon this particular C-47, it is most uncanny that absolutely no human remains were discovered, as though all biological remains were neatly removed. The cause of the fatal accident still remains a mystery 57 years later.

St. Nicholas Magazine, 1890

Trooping fairies on the march

The Fairy Roads of Ireland

Andrew M. Scott
December 2001

Nobody likes to be crossed. Those who hold their lives dear know that if they must cross someone, it should not be someone powerful. The wise also realize that power and size are not synonymous. And so the country people of Ireland, in days gone by, were careful not to offend that group known as "the Little People." It was believed that these mysterious beings could be driven to furious anger by the careless use of their actual names, and so only the most foolhardy would call them by their true title—the fairies. So fearful were people of the power of the Sidh that they would refer to them by even more respectful terms—"the Good People" or "the Gentry."

Despite these congenial appellations, the fairies, though usually out of sight of the mortal world, are depicted in the oft-told tales of Ireland as quite vindictive when crossed. Those men who have had the audacity to interfere with the travels of the race by crossing what is known as a "Fairy Road" have little good to say about the "Good People."

Marching As to War

Irish folklore divides the fairy race into many divisions, each holding unique roles or characteristics. One such sept is known as the *Slua Sidh* or the "trooping fairies." These beings are described as quite small (despite modern imaginings, traditional Irish folklore describes fairies of all heights and builds) and of a particularly martial bent. The trooping fairies were believed to issue magically forth from the thorn-ringed hillocks called "fairy forts." In battalions and companies of both mounted and foot soldiers, they crisscrossed the countryside on hunting expeditions or in search of their invisible enemies.

Few were the mortals who ever saw a host of trooping fairies on the march, but many witnessed the sudden swirls of leaves and hay caused by the great gusts of wind their passing created. Great leaders do not often change their plans once they are afoot. As one might expect, the mighty chieftains of these unseen armies were loath to change the course of their march, and terrible repercussions followed those who disrupted their advance.

The Spectral Carpenters

There is a terrible legend about a man who stood in the way of the fairy troopers. It seems he was a newcomer to the area and was unfamiliar with the fairy road that passed from one fairy fort to another across his land. In fact, the road passed directly through his newly constructed cottage. On their first night in the new dwelling, the man and his family were kept awake by an incessant racket of hammering and sawing, as if a team of carpenters was at work in the house. Searches both within and without the dwelling failed to reveal the source of the noises.

Early the next day, the man went down into the village to ask the advice of his neighbors. He was quickly approached by the local *bean feasa,* or "wise woman."

"You must tear down that house!" she insisted. "The Little People will give you no rest until you do!"

The man had a bit of a temper and was not about to destroy the fine house he had just constructed. He scoffed at her explanation and stormed back to his house.

But night after night the family was tormented by the spectral woodworkers. To add to the man's misery, his wife and children became deathly ill by a mysterious wasting sickness. At last, his family at death's door and his pride crushed, the man came down again to the village to seek out the *bean feasa*. She convinced him at last that the house must come down.

"But what," he asked, "is that terrible racket in my house every night?"

The old woman answered him plainly: "It is the fairies building your coffins."

The house was duly destroyed and a new one constructed in a different location. The family was plagued no more.

Old cottages are found in many parts of Ireland with a corner removed from the building, obviously of later construction. The unusual cut is explained by saying that the offending corner was shorn off to avoid obstructing a fairy road.

How was the builder to know if his planned construction would interrupt the nocturnal jaunt of the local fairy troop? It was the custom in days now past to dig the foundation of a house, then leave off the rest of the construction of the building for a few nights. If the new cottage stood in the

Inside a fairy fort; ring of hedges 60 feet in circumference and 7 feet high.

path of a fairy road, the builders would find their foundation hole filled in the next morning.

I was once told a related story by a man from County Cork in the extreme south of Ireland that supposedly happened to his uncle. This uncle had disregarded local lore and built a stone wall across what was called in those parts a "Funeral Road." This was said to be a path once used by the people of the Great Famine in the 1840s to carry the starvation-ravaged corpses from the village to the mass, unmarked graves used in those tragic times. It was believed that anyone who blocked the funeral road would be plagued by the tormented ghosts of the victims of the Great Famine. My informant's uncle was beset by both deaths in the family and his own eventual madness.

The Stolen Bride

The folk tales of Ireland also depict the trooping fairies interfering with people who have done nothing to them at all, capturing mortals and carrying them along on their sweeping marches down the fairy roads. A typical folk tale of this sort has a young bride dying of a short but mysterious illness, leaving her husband alone in the world. One night as he sits alone in their formerly happy home, he is visited by the specter of his bride. She informs him that she is not, in fact, dead. The fairies had taken a liking to her and had abducted her in the night, replacing her with a changeling that had died and was now in her grave.

Before she disappears, she tells her husband that the only hope of returning her to the land of mortal men is to wait by the fairy road, and when he sees her fly past with the fairy troop, he must stab the black horse she will be astride with an iron knife, thus breaking the spell over her.

The young husband duly arms himself and sits by the fairy road night after night until he at last sees the nearby fairy fort open wide one dark night to belch forth its rushing troop. In their midst is his young wife, atop the swift black horse. She cries to him, but in his fear he hesitates just long enough to doom his happiness. The troop rushes past and his wife is gone forever.

Wise Steeds, Foolish Nobles

Most folklore agrees that a body of trooping fairies was usually invisible to the human senses, a fact that would make travel over unfamiliar ground extremely dangerous. To the rescue came that creature of infinite aid to man, the horse. Of all the animals, the horse is most aware of the passing of the Sidh. Some stories tell us that a passing troop of the Gentry could be seen by human eyes if they were to look directly between the ears of a horse.

But the horse knew it was best to avoid a fairy road, as recounted in the following tale told by my own relations.

My great-grandfather was a coachman to an English lord who visited his lands in Ireland only to collect rent. On one such occasion, my forefather was transporting his aristocratic cargo in a one-horse open carriage. As they approached a nondescript section of road—one often crossed before—the horse came to a dead stop. Unlike a normal horse at rest, this one was frozen in its tracks—not a twitch of the ear nor a flick of the tail. It stood still and silent as if it were constructed of marble.

No amount of whispered persuasion or goading with rein or whip could bring about any change in the animal. The English lord became annoyed at the delay and demanded to know its cause.

"The fairies must be passing on the road before us," was the response of my wise ancestor.

The Englishman would have none of this and climbed down from his cushioned seat to try his own hand at the matter. But no amount of pulling or pushing could move the animal. At last, the exasperated aristocrat returned to his coach and directed the carriage return to his estate. The moment the reins were tugged to the right, the horse awoke from his stupor and trotted home as happy as the day is long.

Some would say that my great-grandfather wanted to stop the collection of the rents, but he swore it was the trooping fairies interrupting their path. And who's to say it wasn't?

Bill Klein at his mine on American Gulch

The Tommyknockers

Bill Klein
May 2002

It was about 50 years ago that I first cut my teeth on mining. I worked as a gold miner in the old Edgar Mine near Idaho Springs, Colorado. Edgar and his men had come from Cornwall in the 1860s. There were still many descendants of the Cornish miners living in the area. I didn't make any money working there, but the experience in learning how to mine would later prove invaluable. I have followed gold mining ever since. Was it there that I first heard of the old Cornish story about the Tommyknockers?

Later I moved to Butte, Montana. Here too there were many descendants of Cornish miners. They brought their skills with them. They also brought the story of the Tommyknockers.

Tommyknockers were little men who lived in the mines. They sometimes played pranks on disbelieving miners. They were known to help out miners who believed in them and showed respect to the wee men. There were stories of miners who were mysteriously warned of impending danger—an explosion perhaps, or maybe a cave-in. When the miner heard a sharp knocking on the mine timbers, he knew that the Tommyknockers were trying to warn him of danger.

Could they have been elves or fairies, or what? Was there any truth to the story the old miners told? We do know that the Bible speaks of angels and ministering spirits. I listened to the stories about Tommyknockers with interest. I did not make fun of the little men. If anything I respected them.

One day in November 1952, my partner and I were walking along a passageway about 3,000 feet below the surface of the ground. Our job was to clean up caved material in a raise in the old Elm Orlu Mine. Then we were to stand timbers and make the raise safe for mining.

As we walked along the passageway, we went by an abandoned tunnel. Peering into the gloom, I suddenly heard a sharp knocking on the mine timbers. "Tommyknockers, pard?" I asked my friend. He just laughed. He was a modern miner and took no stock in superstitious nonsense about little men.

We arrived at the old raise and started to work. By noon we had cleaned up the fallen rock. After lunch we started to stand timbers. We stood two posts. Timbers in the Butte mines have to be big and heavy to take the weight of the rock overhead. I stood up straight to catch my breath. It was exhausting work "timbering up."

"Look out!" my partner yelled. The next second I was flat on my face with stars shooting everywhere. I could not move for the agonizing pain in my right hip, where a 300-pound slab had hit me. Caving rock was falling all around me. At risk to his own life, my partner jumped into the mess and dragged me to safety. Except for him I would not be here now.

They took me by screaming ambulance to old St. James Hospital in Butte. The next day my partner stopped by to see me. He told me that where I had been knocked down, there was now a great pile of caved rock. It would have been my grave. Clearly our Heavenly Father was watching out for me.

I spent a month there. It gave me time to reflect. Ours is a strange world. In the midst of reality we sometimes scoff at the equally strange world of the supernatural. That world, like it or not, sometimes impinges on this one.

Could it be that the Tommyknockers knew that I respected them? Did they then, in turn, try to warn me of impending danger?

Fairy rings of mushrooms were the crop circles of their day.

A Folkloric Herbal

Mark Sunlin
July 2002

Herbs have become increasingly popular in the past few decades. They have brought in billions of dollars annually in various forms—bottled supplements, flavorings, extracts, aromatherapy, cosmetics, insect repellents, and even the natural form of the entire, homegrown, living plant. Yet this pervasiveness is really only a return of their original popularity, for in the past herbs were turned to for all the activities mentioned above, and more. They also figured prominently in folklore. Today, from a modern standpoint, we can re-examine such beliefs. We often find that there was

St. John's wort was believed to reveal hidden spirits.

more behind them in the way of a pharmaceutical or other real-life property to catalyze such beliefs than you might expect from taking these folk legends at face value.

St. John's Wort

Before the 20th century, spirits were believed to have lurked everywhere—in streams, woodlands, gardens, even houses. Yet they were rarely seen and were thus considered to be invisible. "These light and airy spirits have an advantage over slow, unwieldy man in their god-like power of making themselves invisible," observed Jacob Grimm in his *Teutonic Mythology* (1835). "No sooner do they appear than they are snatched from our eyes." Avoiding them was therefore certainly a problem.

However, charms known to the peasant folk were believed to have the power to overcome elfin invisibility, or "glamour," as it was known in Scotland. Foremost among these was a yellow-flowered herb called St. John's wort. Although its reputation is forgotten today, for centuries St. John's wort was a widely valued, glamour-dissolving charm. "Few plants have been in greater demand or invested with such mystic virtues" observed British botanist Thomas Thiselton-Dyer in his 1889 *The Folk Lore of Plants,* remarking on the country folks' belief that the herb allowed them to see otherwise invisible elves, fairies, and witches. On Midsummer's Eve, when unseen spirits were haunting everywhere, windows and doorways throughout Europe were lined with St. John's wort flowers so that the inhabitants would be forewarned of the glamorous unseen presence of any who should enter.

In truth, a tea brewed from St. John's wort did indeed give the impression that it allowed one to see into the spirits' world, for since the early 1900s it has been known among scientists that the plant causes an increased visual sensitivity to bright light called photosensitivity. A modern veterinary text, *The Merck Veterinary Manual,* notes that sheep and cattle will stand in shady areas and blink after browsing on this herb. Similarly, any peasant folk who had brewed a strong tea of St. John's wort would have literally seen the world in a surrealistically new light for a few hours afterwards: The trees, streams, and houses were all where they should be, but now they appeared engulfed in a supernaturally bright, dream-like light, as though sprinkled with fairy dust—or as though the hidden world of elves and wood-nymphs was being revealed. Such imbibers might have become even more receptive psychologically to what they were seeing by a purported antidepressant property associated with this plant. And so the flower power of St. John's wort gained it a reputation as a visual version of Jack's legendary beanstalk—a magic vehicle to the land of ahhs.

Foxglove, like mushrooms, was so alien that it had to be elfin.

Foxglove

For centuries, the alien-looking herb *Digitalis purpurea* has been known in England as "foxglove," a distortion of the name "folks' glove," alluding to the elfin "folk" (as they were often euphemistically called) who were widely believed to have used its colorful, tulip-shaped flowers as gloves and other garments. "Their petticoats are comprised of foxglove, a flower in demand among Irish elves for their gloves, and in some parts of that country for their caps," recorded Thiselton-Dyer of some of the fantasy flower's long-standing associations, adding that "when mending their clothes the foxglove gives them thimbles."

Foxglove doesn't just look alien, it can also kill—a fact quickly blamed on its otherworldly origin. Humans and cattle unfortunate enough to have eaten foxglove leaves suffer heart palpitations and death. However, it is unclear as to whether the peasants believed that elves had deliberately poisoned the foxglove to prevent humans from stealing its attractive flowers, or—perhaps more likely—that its deadliness stemmed simply from its dangerously supernatural origin.

In the long run, it didn't really matter, for either way the danger of the plant became all the more vividly underscored by its connection with the little folk, and the peasants, knowing better than to tamper with anything associated with the spirits' world, learned through word of mouth to leave the folks' glove severely alone. (Even cattle usually avoid it.) Unfortunately, this life-saving lesson has been forgotten, and a few years ago an Oregon couple died after having brewed an herbal tea made of foxglove leaves, unaware of its fatal attraction.

Today, when carefully administered by physicians, the dried, powdered foxglove leaf is used therapeutically to stimulate a weakened heartbeat in the form of a drug called digitalis. Official medical use of foxglove began in 1776, when British physician William Withering discovered its effectiveness from an herbalist known, suitably enough, as "The Witch Woman of Shropshire" (the "witch" designation here meaning only "herbalist").

Ragwort

Although witches are usually pictured flying across the sky on broomsticks, in traditional folklore they were also said to have used a broom-shaped herb called *ragwort* as an aerial vehicle. "Many a man and woman attest to having seen the witches flying on moonlit nights, mounted on the stem of the ragwort," noted Thiselton-Dyer of a report from Cornwall. Elves and fairies, too, were reputed to turn to the ragwort as a means of flight. "It is very rare for traditional fairies to travel by means of wings," observed English Folklore Society president Katharine Briggs in 1976. "They generally fly through the air mounted on transformed ragwort stems or bundles of hay, using them as witches use broomsticks." In Ireland the ragwort was sometimes known as "fairies' horse" because of such beliefs.

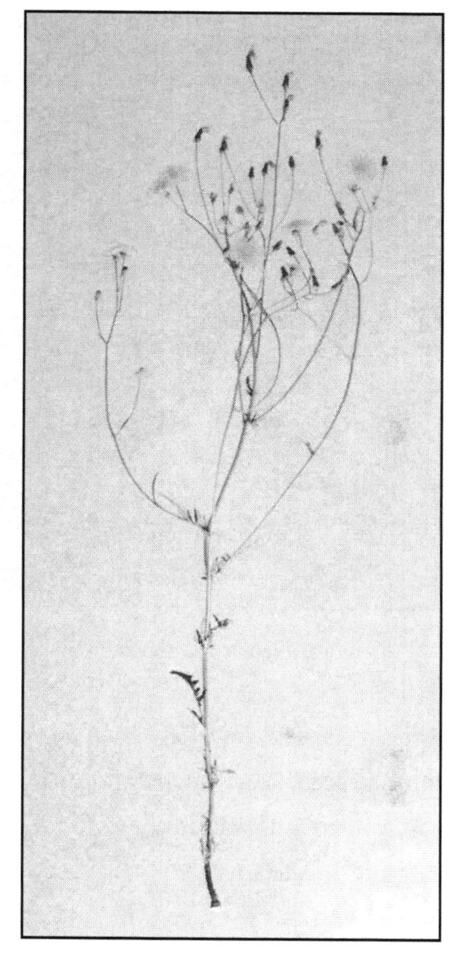

Ragwort, a miniature botanical broomstick in witch lore.

Although native to Europe, the ragwort is now common in North America as well, often growing in untended yards, for it is considered a weed. And it really does resemble a miniature, enchanted broom: Its straight stem is nearly bare, like a broom handle, until it reaches two feet in height, whereupon it bursts into a cluster of 10 to 20 straw-like branches, each tipped by a tiny, dandelion-like flower. In fact, once the suggestion of witchcraft has been made, the impression of an enchanted, botanical broom becomes irresistible.

Aside from its bewitching appearance, the ragwort is poisonous, especially to horses and cattle, who are the only ones likely to eat it in quantities. "Horses and cattle are poisoned by browsing on the tops of these plants,"

The alien growth and appearance of mushrooms connected them with elf lore.

warned Cornell University botanist Walter Muenscher in 1975. Their symptoms, suggestive of witchcraft, show up as "nervous irritability, staggering gait, continuous walking, and sudden appearance of nervous symptoms." A modern veterinary text adds that "some animals become progressively weaker and rarely move, while others wander aimlessly with an awkward gait, either stumbling against or pushing headlong into fences or other structures. Others may become frenzied and dangerously aggressive." Thus, to the peasant folk of yesteryear, they appeared bewitched.

Mushrooms

Mushrooms are mysteriously different from other plants in many ways which once firmly connected them with the world of spirits. They don't look like other plants, for openers, lacking leaves and the familiar green hue of chlorophyll. And they grow in dark forest regions, unlike most sun-loving mortal plants. But most spectacular was their supernaturally swift growth: After a rainfall the woods virtually exploded overnight with mushrooms where the day before there had been none. Knowing only too well how hard it was to coax plants into existence, the peasant folk could only attribute the supernaturally swift growth of these alien-looking mushrooms to the green-thumbed gardening habits of elves, "whose pastime is to make midnight mushrooms," as Shakespeare observed.

Elves and their kin were known to impart a dangerous otherworldliness to anything they were associated with, so it seemed understandable that some mushrooms—"toadstools"—were poisonous.

Mushrooms were sometimes believed to have been sprouted by lightning strikes. This was a surprisingly widespread belief. The Mayan Indians of Mexico and Guatemala believed the red-capped, white-speckled fly agaric mushroom (which is native to both Europe and the Americas) grew where lightning had struck, while in 1850 Irish folklorist Thomas Keightley remarked that the fairy-ring formations of mushrooms were rare in his country, "perhaps on account of the rarity of lightning in Ireland." Actually, this belief isn't as fanciful as it might sound, for mushrooms are dependent on immediate moisture for their rapid sprouting, and thunderstorms certainly provide plenty of that, so it wouldn't be surprising to find mushrooms turning up in connection with such thunder-and-lightning storms—although it is the rain rather than the lightning doing the gardening job.

Fairy Rings

Shakespeare likewise mentioned how the elves "by moonshine do the sour ringlets make, whereof the ewe not bites," and warned of "elves and fairies in a ring, enchanting all that you put in." Among the most mystic of mushroom traits are the "fairy ring" formations of these fungi—groupings of dozens of mushrooms growing together in a mysterious ring-shaped "corral" pattern, usually about six feet in diameter, resembling a miniature, botanical Stonehenge.

These well-ordered geometric growths have such a "tended" look to them that it is tempting, even today, to suspect a supernatural hand behind them.

The peasant folk of yesteryear had no hesitation whatsoever about doing so. To them, these rings marked the paths of fairies and elves who had danced at such locales at night in what was known as a "fairy revel," thus earning these growths their exotic name of "fairy ring," by which the phenomenon is still known to this day. And once that connection had been made their mystique could only increase. It was believed, for example, that stepping into a fairy ring would cause you to become lost in space and time into the supernatural world of the little folk, Rip Van Winkle fashion.

"A fairy ring is enough to surround the mortal with the supernatural condition so that he stands invisible and rapt away from the mortal world which continues all around him," wrote Katharine Briggs, while Thiselton-Dyer remarked that, "When in olden times May dew was gathered by young ladies to improve their complexion, they carefully avoided the grass within fairy rings for fear of displeasing these little beings," adding that "At the present day, the peasant asserts that no sheep or cattle will graze in these mystic patches, a natural instinct warning them of their peculiar origin."

But in reality, Thiselton-Dyer, as a botanist, knew that fairy rings are actually caused by mushrooms sprouting up at the perimeter of their circular, underground root-like mycelium, for mushrooms are only the fruiting section of this main underground plant, just as a flower or berry is to the main body of a bush. Significantly, fairy rings occur only in wild, undisturbed regions. Modern lawn mowers cut mushrooms down before they have a chance to grow into such rings, while in former times sheep, goats, horses, and cattle did the same thing, thereby preventing the formation of fairy rings in all but remote, untrod regions. Of course,this only heightened their mysticism and confirmed the belief of the country folk that such circles were grown by elfin magic.

Witch's Butter

Witch's butter, sometimes known more benignly as "fairy butter," is a bright-yellow, gelatinous fungus related to mushrooms which indeed looks like gobs of butter or yellow Jell-O where it grows on fallen or rotting logs following rains—almost exclusively oak logs, in my experience. This appearance alone was enough to lead peasant folk to believe that such supernatural butter "is made from the roots of old trees." And that is about all that folklorists of the past have recorded about it.

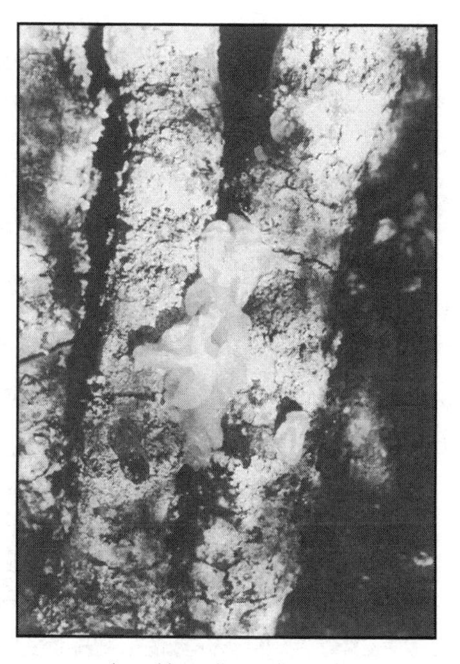

Looking like yellow Jell-O, "fairy butter" grows on oak branches.

The Bloody Alder Tree

White alder trees have a rather curious habit as trees go: They bleed—or *seem* to bleed, anyway. If its bark is cut, the white inner wood of this tree becomes stained deep red in a few minutes. It looks very much as if the tree is bleeding. Once upon a time, this sight caused peoples' imagination to run a little wild, for in his *Teutonic Mythology,* Grimm noted rural beliefs that "when cut, the alder bleeds, weeps, and begins to speak." (An unsettling idea to be sure, since trees are, after all, living things.)

Actually, the bloody substances responsible for this are carotenoids, including the famous beta-carotene, which is better known as a nutritional supplement. Carotenoids account for the orange of today's Halloween Jack-o'-lantern pumpkins and the red of tomatoes and ketchup. They protect living plants from sunlight damage like a botanical sunscreen, and by staining the vulnerable white, exposed inner bark of a damaged alder, carotenoids serve as something of a "botanical bandage" against sunburn.

Even modern scientists can be fooled by this sort of trick. On Lake Superior's Isle Royale National Park, wildlife biologist Durward Allen, who observed the relationships between wolves and moose, spotted a red, "bloody"

An alder branch turns blood-red after being cut.

patch on the snow from an airplane; later, on snowshoeing in to investigate what he expected was the remains of a moose killed and eaten by the wolves, he found instead only moose tracks and red-stained urine on the snow from the carotenoid-rich balsam twigs which the moose had been eating.

Star Jelly

One of the least-known and most colorful of the folkloric beliefs from the European woods was "star jelly." The country folk often saw "falling stars," or meteors, disintegrating as they streaked across the night sky before, sometimes, falling to Earth. At times they would adventurously seek out such unearthly flying objects where they seemed to have landed and found what looked like the remains: a frothy mass of alien-looking gel on grass or other vegetation. In 1678, English novelist John Dryden remarked, "It is a common idea that falling stars are converted into a sort of jelly. I have had the opportunity to see the shooting of stars, and sometimes they appeared as if falling to the ground, where I once or twice found a white, jell-like matter among the grass." As late as 1910, in the scientific journal *Nature*, McKenny Hughes recalled how in his youth in the Welsh countryside he "frequently saw a mass of translucent jelly lying on the ground as if it had been dropped there." Could it have been left by fish-eating birds? he wondered. "But the shepherds knew that such an explanation was inadmissable," he said. "They called it *pwdre ser*—the rot of stars."

Falling stars or spitting trolls were seen behind the frothy foam left on plants by spittlebugs.

Actually, this froth (which can also be found in North America) is something of an "herbal extract" left by the small, leaping insect called the spittlebug *(Philaenus spumarius)*. The adult insects lay their eggs on plants, whereupon the emerging nymphs suck the plant juice to cover themselves with a foamy camouflage against insect-eating birds. (It doesn't really stand out unless you're looking for something unexplainable.) In 1835, Grimm correctly identified the insect responsible, noting that in Germany the froth was "cockoo-spit," and in Norway "troll-spit," being attributed to the foul-smelling, cave-dwelling "Bigfoot" of the Germanic evergreen woods.

Mistletoe

Mistletoe rings a bell to everyone as a Christmas decoration, yet even then it is more commonly heard of than actually seen, or even recognized. It is in fact, a simple vine-like plant, without any pointedly mystic properties—except one: It grows not from out of the ground like normal plants,

Mistletoe remains green all year when the tree it grows from is bare, giving it a mystical allure.

but from the upper branches of trees. This becomes especially evident during the winter months when the "host" tree loses its leaves to reveal the vine-like mistletoe draping itself decoratively with its leaves remaining green year-round.

Some 2,000 years ago mistletoe was at the height of its supernatural status among European Celts, as Greek scholar Pliny recorded at the time: "The Druids (for so they call their magicians) hold nothing more sacred than the mistletoe and the tree on which it grows, provided only it be an oak." In 1911, California folklorist W. Y. Evans-Wentz explained in his doctoral thesis, published as *The Fairy Faith in Celtic Countries*, and written while he was a post-graduate student in Britain, that "The Celts may have viewed the mistletoe as the secret of the tree's life, because during the winter sleep of the leafless oak the mistletoe maintains its own foliage, and like the heart of a sleeper continues pulsing with vitality. The mistletoe was thus regarded as the heart center of the divine spirit of the oak."

Mountain Ash

"No tree, perhaps, holds such a prominent place in witchcraft lore as the mountain ash, its mystic power having rarely failed to ward off their spells," observed Thiselton-Dyer of long-standing folk beliefs. "So potent is the ash as a counter-charm to sorcery that even the smallest twig renders their actions impotent." Mountain ash trees—also known as rowan trees—were sometimes planted near houses as protection from witches, he noted, while in

Germany, Denmark, and Norway "rowan branches are usually put over stable doors to keep out witches."

Katharine Briggs remarked that "the red berries of the rowan made it specially effective against witchcraft and fairies' spells," noting that red berries were often regarded (for some reason) as being protective against supernatural spells. She was probably right about the berries, but not about the color as being the foundation. The mountain ash's reputation stems more likely from a sugar called sorbitol, which abounds in its berries.

A gastric irritant, moderately high levels of sorbitol produce a gripping action to the digestive tract, which results in a laxative-purgative effect similar to that suffered from eating too many prunes. In fact, it is the ten-percent sorbitol level in prunes which gives that fruit its famous laxative effect. The ash is so rich in sorbitol that its berries were the original commercial source of this sugar, which even takes its name from the scientific name for the mountain ash—*Sorbus.*

To this day, warnings on the labels of chewing gum and breath mints containing the sugar of this anti-witchcraft tree caution imbibers to avoid overindulgence or suffer the trots. In days of old, for similar reasons, the peasant folk must have felt that witches would suffer a similar loss of their magic power when confronted by the tree—or as an English ballad chanted, "Witches have no power where there is rowan-tree wood." (It is curious that the peasantry viewed this property as making the tree a charm in their favor, rather than as evidence that it had been poisoned by witches or goblins. But as Katharine Briggs noted, "The last thing to expect in folk tradition is consistency.")

A fairy house.

A State-Sponsored Fairy Village

Janet Brennan
February 2003

Once upon a time, there sat a magical island off the coast of Maine. This island, Mackworth by name, comprised 100 acres—a nice, round number, as round as the island itself, as round as a fairy ring.

A foot trail just over a mile in length ran all around the edge of this island, encircling its deep, cool woods and skirting the tops of the rocky seaside cliffs that glowed golden in the sun. In the center of the island, beneath the

Carved faces flank the "ear" on the interior of the Listening Tree. Deaf children communicated to the tree by signing to the faces.

cathedral pines, was another circle, this one made of stone. The stone circle was built by the island's owner, a good, kind governor of Maine, Percival Baxter, a man who loved nature as much as he loved animals and people. Gov. Baxter lived on the island in a fine house with his beloved Irish setters. Inside the circular wall of rock he laid to rest his cherished pets when they passed into the world of spirits, until eventually the circle contained the bones of 19 Irish setters and one horse.

The circle of seasons turned round and round, until finally came the day when Gov. Baxter himself passed into spirit. As his legacy, he bequeathed his wonderful island to the state, ordering the government to preserve it as a "sanctuary for wild beasts and birds." He also left over half a million dollars for the state to build a causeway connecting Mackworth Island to the mainland, and for the state to build a boarding school for deaf children on the island, the only such school in the state.

Home for Deaf Children

The Listening Tree, used by generations of students at the Gov. Baxter School for the Deaf.

Now, instead of the island being enjoyed only by the Baxter family and their pets, it became a home and refuge for deaf schoolchildren, as well as "wild beasts and birds." The children explored its woods and beaches, and found on the edge of the island a tree that was more special than the rest. A casual observer would consider this tree dead, as it was little more than a sun-bleached pillar of smooth wood, with half of it fallen away, exposing its empty interior. But the children knew appearances can deceive, and sometimes what seems dead is only silent. They could see that an old knothole looked like a giant ear, and the children who knew how to speak began to whisper their secrets into it.

But what of the deaf children who could not talk to the "listening tree"? Were they to be deprived of sharing confidences with this patient friend? No, ever resourceful, they carved faces into the tree's hollow interior, so that they could talk to the tree in sign language, and the wise old tree would see them signing and understand.

Again the circle of seasons turned round, and as more deaf children began getting services in their local school systems, fewer came to live at the Gov. Baxter School for the Deaf on Mackworth Island. But the island exerted its lure on residents of the mainland, enticing them to walk their dogs to the pet cemetery or jog past the "listening tree" along the seaside perimeter. Eventually the state built a parking lot to accommodate the many visi-

Mackworth Island, Maine, with the causeway connecting it to the mainland on the left.

tors, yet the island lost none of its natural beauty, or its magic.

One day, in the summer of 2002, a children's book author from New Hampshire came to Maine to promote her book, *Fairy Houses,* at a bookstore near Mackworth Island. Tracey Kane's book, published in 2001, tells how children on Maine islands traditionally have built secret houses for fairies, using only non-living things found in nature. The bookstore was expecting only a few dozen people to come meet the author, but instead, several hundred showed up. Such is the lure of fairies.

Fairies Settle on Mackworth

A local woman whose own daughters had been building fairy houses in their backyard suggested the author lead a fairy-house workshop on nearby Mackworth Island. So, after getting permission from the Baxter School and the Maine Department of Conservation, which oversees the island, hundreds of people trooped over the causeway to build fairy houses on Mack-

On a September morning, a father and son work on a house in the fairy village.

worth.

Parents thought their children would forget about their fairy houses after this one-day building spree. But the little ones seemed to be under a magical spell. Again and again they begged their parents to take them to the island, so they could check to see if any fairies had yet taken up residence in their new homes. Some children did see signs of success and gratitude from the fairies, such as a tiny bouquet of flowers left at a door, or sparkly fairy dust sprinkled on a roof. Other little home-builders found no signs of habitation, so they returned again and again to add more decorations to their houses or build bigger and better ones.

As the building boom on the island continued throughout that summer and fall, the state decided to give official recognition to the fairy housing development. The Department of Conservation's Bureau of Parks and Land erected a large sign in the woods, surely the most unusual sign ever erected by a government bureau. It reads: "Welcome to Mackworth Island Community Village. You may build houses small and hidden for the fairies, but please do not use living or artificial materials. The best materials are found in the landscape of the village itself, but if you chose to bring in natural materials, please return with those that you didn't use. Thank you for treating the island with care and respect. This helps keep the fairies coming back!"

There are now dozens and dozens of fairy houses in the village. They are made of twigs, leaves or driftwood, and are decorated with feathers, flowers, seashells, pebbles, and pine cones. Most nestle among the roots of trees, while some are built at child-height in the branches. There are so many houses, they are starting to encroach on Governor Baxter's Irish setter cemetery.

And still the children come and build. Their parents also fall under the spell of the addictive activity. But, as in all human endeavors, naysayers come forward. Some fairy-house purists have written letters to the editor of the local newspaper, complaining that the houses are too large and visible to really attract fairies. True Maine fairy houses, they say, are tiny, hidden things that only a fairy can see.

I once had the magical experience of stumbling across one such fairy house. Years ago, while hiking on a nature trail with my children, I happened to notice something odd at the foot of a tree. Upon closer inspection, I found it was three small, wooden blocks set up to form three walls, with the fourth side left open as an entrance. It was topped with another wooden block for a roof. The whole thing was covered with pieces of moss, making it almost invisible against the forest floor. Not being native New Englanders, we were clueless as to why anyone would build such a thing. Was it for chipmunks, or for fairies? The years passed, my children grew up, and the little house fell into disarray; the moss dead, the blocks on their sides. Finally one day I noticed all traces of the house were gone. Only the mystery of its builder remains.

As for Mackworth Island, are the fairies happy with their village there? I think so. They can watch the innocent children working so diligently along-

A fairy house abuts a log.

side their parents to create something nice for a creature none of them may ever see. They can hear the secrets still whispered to the "listening tree," and the murmer of the sea breeze as it dances through the lush pines. They can feel the spirits of the faithful Irish setters standing guard over this special, mystical place. Surely all the spirits of Mackworth Island—the wild beasts and birds, the children and the fairies—will live happily ever after.

The Back Beyond

Paranormal Mysteries of the Superstition Mountains

Stan Morrison
June 2003
Photographs and Special Research by Linda Morrison

In early 1991, I was enjoying a six-day solo hiking excursion in the Four Peaks Wilderness of south-central Arizona when I happened upon an unexpected mystery on a trail at around the 6,000 foot level. I was 7 for 7,657-foot Brown's Peak, the tallest and farthest west of the Four Peaks, and my mind was very far from anything unusual. I was in the habit (and still am) of examining the tracks of the wildlife that cross my path; e.g., white-tailed

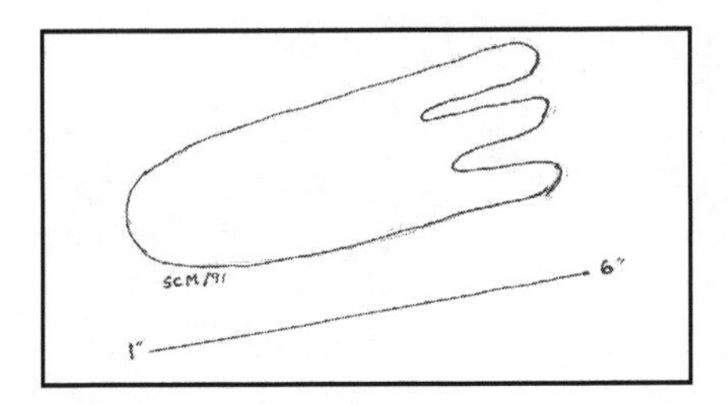

Strange track observed by author near the Four Peaks in 1991.

deer, mountain lion, bobcat.

I was keeping my eyes open for black bear tracks—this wilderness being the largest concentration of black bear in Arizona—when I came upon a print made by something that certainly is unknown to science.

A Strange Footprint

It was on an exposed boulder covered with a thin layer of dust. The track, or print, was approximately six inches long and looked something like a small human print, but it had only three toes. Apparently, it had walked out of the evergreen and stepped on the exposed dust-covered rock. There was only one print, and apparently it (the animal) entered the evergreen forest on the other side of the trail. I took one photograph, but unfortunately the print did not show up.

It was a nice hike, and when I reached the craggy summit of Brown's Peak I was fascinated and amused at some of the graffiti, one example dating back to 1849. I spent several hours on the peak viewing the surrounding lakes. It was a breathtaking panorama. To the east and far below, I could see the entire Superstition Mountains. Weaver's Needle was clearly visible, and I received the impression that I was looking at a bunch of dunes. All of the mountains seemed uniform in size. But the reality is that they are not and the peak on which I was standing was actually a geological extension of the Superstition range, only a thousand feet higher than the other mountains.

What kind of creature made that print back at the 6,000-foot level on the trail? And what connection could such a creature have with the reportedly mysterious nature of the Superstition Mountains?

I think it is safe to say that the six-inch, three-toed footprint I found in the Four Peaks Wilderness was not made by an eight-foot sasquatch.

A Race of Pygmies?

I have thought a lot about that three-toed track since 1991, and it has been easy for me to imagine that such a small creature could easily adapt to both the low-elevation Sonoran scrub and the higher-elevation evergreen forests.

But is there any corroborating information that such creatures are known to occur in the Superstitions and surrounding areas?

Gary Jennings devotes a chapter in his 1973 book, *The Treasure of the Superstition Mountains,* to the bizarre legends and enigmatic stories of the region. It seems there are local Native American beliefs that may relate to whatever left that small, three-toed footprint:

"Another of the Pima legends is that the Superstitions were at one time 'guarded' by a race of pygmies. This could possibly be a tribal memory of the Hohokam. The few bones found by anthropologists hint that 'they who went away' were an elfin race, in general around five feet tall. That is well beyond pygmy height, but they would have been small even beside the squat-built Pimas."

There are a number of other stories of ancient lost tribes in the Superstition Mountains. I must admit that entities reported with only three toes are absent, as is a coat of fur or hair. On the other hand, there is a spring in the Superstitions officially named "Monkey Spring."

Archetypal Events

Other paranormal investigators, during the course of interviewing and examining significant locations, will be confronted with inconsistencies or high-strangeness phenomena that can cause a great deal of confusion.

I'm convinced that the more popular phenomena, such as UFOs and Bigfoot, have become archetypal and that some of their appearances take place in the psychic realm. When conditions are just right they become material projections. While these phenomena are generally short-lived, the nuts-and-bolts UFOs are fixed and continue to be seen and photographed by the

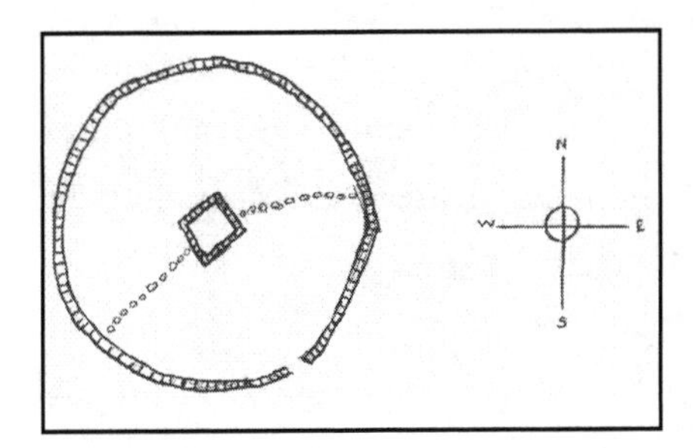

Circlestone, Superstition Mountains.
Circumference approximately 427 feet.

thousands. Biological Bigfoot/sasquatches continue to be observed, often leaving behind strange and/or huge footprints as evidence of their passing.

Even though solid and biological phenomena likely venture into the Superstitions, various psi manifestations are probably more often experienced, since the Superstition Mountains themselves have become mythical and archetypal.

Jennings notes the mysterious and eerie nature of the Superstition Wilderness: "Ghoulies, ghosties, things that go bump in the night...From the first primitives who came here, to the latest flying saucer nuts, everybody has been inspired by the weird atmosphere of the Superstitions..."

Skinwalkers

John Green has written that he tends to steer clear of many of the Arizona reports of Bigfoot creatures because of the "skinwalkers" of several Arizona Indian tribes. Usually, Arizona skinwalkers are medicine men, or shamans, of the Hopi, Navajo, or various Apache tribes. Ritualistically, they don furs or hides of wolves or coyotes and roam about at night. In their religious fervor they believe they can take on the mental cunning and physical agility and endurance of the wolf or coyote. Practically all Native Americans in Arizona are not only aware of the skinwalker practice, but believe it is a currently active ritual.

I own a plaster bust of a skinwalker wearing the hide of a wolf or coyote and a beaded necklace the centerpiece of which is a large peyote button. It has long been known that the ingestion of peyote often plays a major role in religious rituals of Amerindians of the Southwest. A hallucinogen would certainly enhance the skinwalker practice.

A large part of Circlestone lays in scattered and collapsed disarray.

I can't deny that a skinwalker could be mistaken for a Bigfoot, especially at night. But I don't believe that a skinwalker would leave behind a footprint with only three toes.

Circlestone

The inhospitality and majesty of the Superstition Mountains really must be experienced to be appreciated. The elevation varies from 1,800 feet in lower Boulder Canyon to Mound Mountain at 6,262 feet above sea level. In this Wilderness Area, which currently encompasses 242 square miles, temperatures can reach a sweltering 130 degrees in the summer. In the winter, regions can attain a numbing 10 degrees below zero. It is here, in such harsh conditions, that ancient peoples constructed ingenious habitations (140 major archaeological sites exist in the Superstition Wilderness). Near the highest elevation of the Superstitions, these peoples constructed a very interesting artifact over a thousand years ago. It is known today as "Circlestone."

I had long heard that a "medicine wheel" (ancient archaeoastronomical

The remains of the central cairn at Circlestone.

ruin) existed in the Superstition Mountains. But it wasn't until the first week of May 2001 that Linda and I hiked the 11 rugged miles to the site. Though we ourselves examined the remote artifact, the chief source of the story of the ruin is James A. Swanson and Thomas J. Kollenborn's 1986 book, *Circlestone: A Superstition Mountain Mystery* (Goldfield Press). It is from this excellent publication that we drew our specific information pertaining to the site.

It was an arduous week-long trek to Circlestone, but it was both enjoyable and fruitful. When we reached Circlestone after scaling the 6,010-foot ridge, we both were elated.Now it was time to survey and photograph this mysterious ruin, an artifact that could be as important as England's Stonehenge.

Unfortunately, when we reached the site, we found that a great deal of the outer wall had collapsed and there were areas of sandstone blocks strewn about in piles. In the early investigations of Circlestone, measurements and important cosmic alignments were recorded. But when we examined the circular ruin, it would have been almost impossible to reproduce the astronomical alignments because of the crumbling condition of the site.

We spent about four hours at Circlestone, and we later agreed that the remaining walls seemed similar to ruins of sandstone block walls in Chaco Canyon in New Mexico. These specific walls were also built without the use of mortar, and the intrepid builders were the ancient Anasazi.

Surveys of Circlestone

Kollenborn first made accurate measurements of Circlestone between 1963 and 1975 and was the first researcher to bring scientists and archaeologists to the site, where they confirmed that it was a prehistoric Indian ruin

Fish Creek Canyon. Somewhere in the canyons of Fish Creek exists the entrance to an underground UFO base, according to novelist and contactee Kay Kizziar.

and not a corral for goats or sheep. The sandstone blocks used at the site are referred to as "two-man blocks," since their size required two men to raise and put them in place.

Based on Kollenborn's meticulous survey, Dr. Malcolm Comeaux, Professor of Arizona Geography at Arizona State University, and Sam Henderson, the Park Superintendent at Casa Grande National Monument, became actively involved in further Circlestone investigation in 1981. The scientists were in agreement that Circlestone indeed recorded astronomical events and was a sacred site to the builders.

Kollenborn felt that the narrow, three- foot-wide doorway probably acted as a frame to capture the sun, sending it to a precise location or direction to identify a celestial event. Dr. Henderson reported:

"At precisely noon on June 21, the summer solstice, the sun did indeed shine directly through the outer door and align perfectly with the interior door. This is the first day of the calendrical summer, an event of tremendous significance to early agrarian cultures."

Who Built It?

As of now, the question is no longer what the function of Circlestone is, but who exactly built the structure in the first place. The experts have narrowed the builders down to either the Salado or the Anasazi and believe it was built 1,700 years ago.

In *Circlestone*, the authors devote a chapter to "Dubious Theories." Even though Kollenborn has written about anomalous lights in the Superstitions in the past, in the Circlestone book he and Swanson examine a possible UFO connection somewhat lightly. They write as follows:

"Since the publication of *Chariots of the Gods* by Erich Von Däniken, many individuals have surmised that Circlestone was a high marker built for extraterrestrial use. The people who espouse this theory believe that many circular ruins of similar size throughout the world were (or perhaps are) guides for spaceships visiting Earth. Each year unidentified flying object sightings are reported. Most turn out to be identified or explained, but about 10 percent remain a mystery. The Superstition Wilderness has not been overlooked when it comes to alleged UFO sightings."

Many UFO Reports

"During the late 1950s and early 1960s many reports of UFO sightings circulated in Apache Junction. Unofficially, UFOs have been seen throughout the Superstition Wilderness, and there are many alleged eyewitness accounts from which to choose. According to the number and locations of 'sightings,' a favorite spot for UFOs is the top of Superstition Mountain near the Flat Iron and in the Bluff Springs Mountain area. Also, there have been reports of UFO sightings near Mound Mountain adjacent to Circlestone.

"During the winter of 1973, two men were camped at Reavis Ranch. Both men claimed to have observed a UFO landing and taking off from the Circlestone site. One man said he saw the spaceship land and several small, green individuals disembark. According to the storyteller, the creatures later got back on board, and the craft departed in a giant flash of light.

"An old cowboy once related the story of a circular burned spot in the Superstitions. He said much of the surface rock around the burned circle had been melted, as though something had once accelerated in a vertical direction very rapidly, producing a tremendous amount of heat. Another individual told of a burned spot where he found three pad marks that were left by a craft that landed and then took off very quickly. When asked why he did not report his findings, he laughed and replied, 'I like riding in the mountains too well to spend several months in an institution.'

"Most people who have lived and worked around the Superstitions, however, have never seen a UFO—or at least are not telling anybody about it."

Canyon Lake UFOs

A friend of mine, Randy Daniels, 41, an electrician by trade, was parked with a friend around ten years ago in the early morning hours near the boating dock of Canyon Lake. They were standing outside their pickup taking in the spectacular, star-filled sky when all of a sudden out of Boulder Canyon (in the western Superstitions), a huge white ball of light shot from the canyon, crossed above them at several hundred feet, and continued at a tremendous speed to the west. It seemed to shoot farther into the dark sky until they lost sight of it over a large hill on the other side of the lake. It frightened the two so badly that they immediately jumped into their truck and went home. According to Randy, it was definitely something anomalous and spectacular rather than merely an interesting light in the sky. This is not the first time such a huge bright light has been seen leaving Boulder Canyon in such a manner.

When Linda and I returned from Circlestone to our base camp near the old Reavis Ranch, we lay in our sleeping bags and took in the awe-inspiring beauty of the star-filled sky. At 9:00 P.M., May 9, 2001, I pointed out to

Canyon Lake, not far from Boulder Canyon. There have been a number of UFO sightings around this lake.

Linda three white lights very high up and coming from the north, west, and south all at the same time. These were not airplanes and were dimmer than the background stars. As we watched, they crossed the sky and from those opposite directions came together high in the sky directly above us. There was a short hesitation, and they then continued on their course until they were out of sight. When I later asked Linda her thoughts about the lights, her comment was, "It appeared as it was definitely planned how they came together and met each other...I don't know what they were...I had never seen anything like that."

A great deal more field work needs to be conducted on the strange phenomena occurring in the Superstition Wilderness. Interested parties with access to modern (and exotic) technology designed to record, detect, measure, and otherwise help us further understand paranormal and anomalous phenomena in this wilderness would be a valuable asset to the investigation. Perhaps slowly but surely the mysteries of the Superstition Mountains will become a little less mysterious.

The region is a rough but wonderful area to conduct paranormal research. The experience of the Superstition Mountains alone makes any expedition memorable and definitely worthwhile.

Little People

Donald Taylor
August 2003

One bright Sunday afternoon last summer, I lay on the living-room sofa to take a nap. All the windows and the front door, which I lay facing, were open, with the screen latched. I dozed lightly and would have heard anyone who might have come up on the front porch, as would my Yorkie, Scarlett O'Hara.

When I awakened about half an hour later, the white tile in front of the door was smeared with an enormous amount of what appeared to be blood. Having long since resigned myself to not being startled by such phenomena, the only thing that worried me was the thought that Scarlett might have been bleeding. I immediately checked her all over and found nothing. I tried wiping the "blood" up with a paper towel, but it was as dry as a coat of paint. A damp sponge, however, removed it easily.

The same thing happened again recently, although this time the substance was a much smaller amount. Unlike the movies, the unexplained in real life does not always happen at two in the morning accompanied by crashing thunder and flashes of lightning.

This past winter, Scarlett awakened me one morning about four to take her out. It had been snowing for several hours. No cars had come by on our quiet street, and no humans had been abroad in the night, leaving the several inches of snow as undisturbed as the icing on a wedding cake. But *something* had been out.

A set of small round footprints, about an inch in diameter, started in the very middle of the driveway, led down the walk, and ended right in the center of my front porch. No tracks led to or from the places where this set of tiny, perfectly shaped tracks began and ended. I joked to a friend that perhaps it was Death, and when he got to the porch, he looked at the address and said, "Oops, wrong house!"

Several weeks ago, I was in the kitchen making potato salad. I put the lid back on a jar of pimientos and closed it tightly, leaving it sitting on the counter. A couple of minutes later, the lid came flying off the jar, sailed across my head, and landed on the stove. This has happened again, and somehow a tall, slender aluminum pot, which contains an arrangement of dried flowers and is weighted down with gravel in the bottom, has managed to fall over twice in my bedroom.

But nothing can top my encounters with the "little people." One night a few weeks ago, I was reading in bed before going to sleep. My magazine was on the floor, and I was lying on my stomach with my head hanging over the side of the bed—my usual reading position. I saw movement near the foot of the bed out of the corner of my eye.

As I looked up, this tiny little woman—about two feet tall—walked the length of my bed, stepped on the magazine, and said, "Excuse me!" Then she walked between the bed and the night table and simply disappeared. She was really cute—she had curly red hair and was wearing a little housedress patterned with pink, blue, and yellow flowers. I would have given anything if she would have stopped so we could have talked for a few minutes.

A few days later, again in the kitchen, I was preparing some food when I again saw motion in the breakfast alcove. Looking around, I saw a tiny little man—probably the little woman's husband—standing under the table. He was dressed all in brown, from boots to hat. His hat had a rather large feather stuck in the brim. He winked and gave me a smart little salute, then disappeared.

Whether these adorable little beings really do inhabit the same world as we—and I would like to hope that they do—or whether they live in a parallel universe which a few of us are blessed to glimpse for a brief moment, I would not presume to speculate. But the encounter was exhilarating.

The Bush

Douglas W. Cracraft
September 2003

Several years ago, I was deeply involved in New Age interests, having steeped myself in *The Magic of Findhorn*, books by Ruth Montgomery, automatic writing, and books by psychics on nature spirits, as well as drinking mystical herbal tea. I had also begun meditating during my lunch breaks. I would take a campstool to an old truck lane behind the building I worked in, and facing the uncleared tract of land, I would close my eyes and consciously attempt to slow my mental activity to the alpha frequency.

One day, as I was floating deeper into mental relaxation and tranquility, an unbidden thought suddenly popped into my mind that perhaps I was ready to communicate with nature spirits, in whom I devotedly believe. As soon as that thought occurred to me, I was startled by a sudden loud, frantic rattling, as if dozens of castenets were being played simultaneously. Opening my eyes in alarm, I saw directly in front of me a large bush, with each of its numerous branches shaking violently.

I nearly fell backward off my stool, as I heard—again in my head—the sound of playful laughter. With the laughter was an amused voice that told me, "Yeah, you're ready all right!"

I later told a friend of my experience and took her back to the same location. But I could not find the bush anywhere. Even now, the image of that bush is burned into my memory, but despite searching up and down that tract of land, I never saw that bush again.

A Gift from the Birds

Twilight Bard
October 2003

New York City was dark under storm clouds pelting the streets with snow, and the damp wind clutched the body with an icy grip. I was exhausted from the single mother's daily grind, feeling like I had been running on fumes all winter. After spending all my energy trudging downtown to be met with an empty classroom and a "Cancelled" sign displayed on the door, I was vexed.

With hours to kill, I decided to head for the nearby Botanical Gardens, where I often sat by the pond and fed the birds. I figured a bench in a warm greenhouse would make for a cozier study place than the dreary college cafeteria.

I entered the front gates and began making my way down the untrodden white path. Not far in, among the snow-laden evergreens and ice-sparkling branches, I felt I had been transported to another world. Within moments, the breeze softened and the clouds passed, leaving a clear blue sky.

I followed the path to the edge of a frozen pond. Just as I passed a tree, a blue jay landed on a bough level with my face, just a couple of feet away, and cawed at me. I stopped moving, and the shiny black eyes of the bird met mine.

Now, Blue Jay is my totem animal, so I pay attention when I see one, especially when it so blatantly calls to me. The Blue Jay represents the connection between the Earth and the heavens, and that connection was definitely something I had been lacking in my busy life.

Another jay arrived and landed on the tree, and then another. Then some chickadees landed on the ground, just inches from my feet. Ducks began to waddle off the frozen pond toward me. I stood as still as possible while cardinals, ravens, pigeons, blackbirds, robins, mourning doves, sparrows, and host of other feathered friends I couldn't identify flocked in a circle around me. Some perched on branches, some hopped along the ground, some even circled in the air overhead.

They chirped and cawed, quacked and cooed, and I was mesmerized by the rhythm of their chorus. My mind began to drift as I became lost in the moment. I felt some pricking on the back of my neck; then slowly my senses began to tingle. It felt as though I were standing in a field of static electricity, sort of like when you rub a balloon on your head and make your hair stand on end.

A surge of energy seemed to run up my spine with the crescendo of chatter. It reached a climax, and then in a thunderous burst of pounding wings, the birds dispersed into the four winds, leaving me there alone, renewed, with nothing but a few discarded feathers to reassure myself that it really happened.

Nature's blessings are abundant; sometimes we need only to stand still to receive them.

My Encounter with the Little Man

Ron Quinn
May 2004

This strange occurence took place during August 1942 in Mongaup Valley, a small community located several miles east of Monticello in upstate New York. Even today, 56 years later, this event is as fresh in my mind as if it had happened only last week.

Each summer, our parents would take my brother Chuck and me on a two-week vacation somewhere in New York. Mom's older sister would accompany us with her three children: Martin, Jackie, and Rita. Our dad would come out during the weekend for a visit, then return home by train.

These little escapes to the country were a welcome change after spending almost a year in the cramped confines of the city. We would either head for the mountains or rent a beach cottage out on Long Island. Most of these vacations were filled with adventures, especially if our cousins were along.

Dad had met Richy Murtagh through a friend, and Murtagh mentioned his folks had acreage and a large home in Mongaup Valley, and also a guest cottage they rented out for the summer months. Dad asked if they would rent him the place for several weeks, because he was searching for a place to send the family for vacation. Dad also said that Mom's sister would most likely come along with her children. Richy checked with his parents and they agreed to rent us the cottage.

Unknown to me at the time, this vacation and the strange experience I would encounter would stay with me for the rest of my life.

Murtagh met us at the train, and how we all managed to squeeze into his car with all our baggage is another mystery. It was about eight miles to his place, and as we sped along, my heart beat with excitement at the prospect of living out in the open country once more before school began.

Murtagh mentioned that a river that had a deep swimming area was near the cottage. In a short while we crossed a bridge, and I caught sight of the river below.

Turning right, we traveled a short distance along a dirt road, then up a hill. On the right stood a large, stately, two-story home surrounded by trees. Just below was the cottage, near an open field. A cow grazed nearby and the family dog, Nelly, barked wildly as we came to a stop.

Our first enjoyable afternoon was spent exploring the surrounding country. I ran happily down the grassy slopes and felt the cool grass beneath my bare feet. The air had a clean freshness to it as I stopped beside the river and sat with the others, dangling my feet in the cool, moving water.

Several days into our vacation, which at times resembled a Tom Sawyer adventure, especially our trips along the river, I committed a minor infraction of the laws set down by Mom and was instructed to return to the cottage and remain there for an hour while the others played.

A Small Visitor

I was sitting perhaps four feet from a window. After a short period of time, I heard a tapping sound, like somebody gently hitting a nail against glass. I looked in the direction of the sound and froze in fear. Standing on the outside window ledge was a small, oddly dressed man about 12 inches high.

At this point, you might be saying, "Oh, just a young child's imagination." But not so.

This little fellow did not entirely resemble the traditional elf, gnome, or leprechaun we have all seen depicted in various books and movies. Somewhat frightened, especially by something I knew could not exist, I looked away in hopes the illusion would disappear.

Again came the sound, and once more I glanced up. The little guy was smiling and waving his hand. The tapping came from his walking stick tapping lightly against the windowpane.

After all these years, I can still describe that little man, down to the last detail, as his image is branded deep in my memory. He had an odd-looking hat, dark green in color. A short, dark gray beard covered his lower face. From beneath his hat, silky, curly hair cascaded down to his shoulders and covered his ears, which I never saw.

His light gray shirt fit somewhat tightly around his upper body, but the sleeves were quite baggy. The little guy's trousers were the same color and ended just below the knee. Something resembling a black belt encircled his wide waist, but it had no buckle. He wore dark brown, soft-looking boots that ended just below the trousers. The toes of his footwear did not curl back and end in a point like we have seen in drawings.

Comparing his features to those of a normal-size man, he looked to be in his 50s. His extremely large eyes were his most striking feature, and the expression on his little face was that of pure friendship and love.

I sat gazing at this individual in dismay. I might have been only a lad of ten, but I had been told many times I was several years ahead of myself when it came to logical thinking. I knew what I was seeing just couldn't exist.

Now I understand children of this age have some vivid imaginations and often see things that aren't really there. The excitement of the trip, the dark, lonely forests, and all the fun we were having could have triggered an illusion like this, but what I was looking upon was real in every sense of the word, including the movement of his body and the shadow he cast on the ledge below. Everything was there.

After a few moments, this happy fellow motioned for me to come closer. I glanced out another window and saw the others playing with Nelly. I wanted to open the door and call to them, but changed my mind for no apparent reason. I looked back toward the little guy, and again he motioned for me to come nearer. This time I did, and knelt beside the window a foot or so from my uninvited guest.

He kept smiling and looking me over as if he had never been this close to a human before. When I first saw him I had experienced fear. Now my feelings had turned to bewilderment and friendship, mixed with a dab of sadness.

I didn't speak, but simply knelt transfixed at what I was witnessing. I reached forward and slowly opened the window. As I reached out to touch this strange individual that had invaded my life, he stepped back and his head tilted from left to right as he inspected me from every angle.

After smiling once more, the little guy leaped from the ledge, landing gracefully on the grass below. He ran with long leaps across the lawn, stopping momentarily to look back, then disappeared among the shadows of the trees.

I ran and told the others, but they only laughed, as I might have if I heard the same tale from another. Mom smiled and said I was either daydreaming or had a very active imagination.

A Memory and a Mystery

The others went on to tease me for several days about my tall tale. Occasionally, while out hiking with the gang, one would stop and yell out, "Look...look! I just saw that little man run across the path!" Then they would all run off laughing.

During the last week, I always kept an eye out for that little fellow, but I never saw him again.

Dad was an artist and I inherited his talent, so I drew a sketch of my little visitor. I still have the original.

In 1946 we moved from New York to Washington State, then to Tucson, Arizona.

In all this time, that one experience remains high on my list of pleasant memories. I've told this story numerous times at parties and so on and have received various explanations.

To this day I'm certain that strange little character was real and not something conceived in the mind of a young lad with a "very active imagination," as Mom had put it.

Why am I so certain, you might ask.

Well, the final proof was the little footprint left in the soft earth just below the window. When the fellow jumped, one foot landed on the grass while the other hit the moist ground. It left a perfect print, but the others claimed I had made it to try to prove my story.

It's quite possible none of this ever happened. If that is the case, why have these few moments of fantasy been so cemented into my memory? Either it happened or it didn't. There can be no middle ground. This brings to mind another well-known statement: "There are more things in heaven and earth than are dreamt of in your philosophy."

Seeing Fairies

Rosemary Ellen Guiley
November 2004

Folklore holds that fairies cannot be seen or noticed in any way unless they want you to observe them. That's true to some extent, but developing "fairy sight," the ability to perceive fairies, is easier than one might think. In this article I'll share with you some of my fairy experiences, and how I've increased my ability to notice them.

Who Are the Fairies?

Fairies include a wide range of beings who populate nature and live in homes and buildings. Many people think fairies are tiny beings with wings, but they come in all shapes and sizes, from small balls of light to little humanoid beings to towering, angelic figures. There are different races of fairies, just as there are different races of humans. The fairy realm includes nature spirits and elementals, household helpers, worker beings, guardians of the land, spirits who live in man-made machines, and overlighting presences who hold and nourish the archetypal patterns of all species.

Fairies are powerful beings. According to lore, they work tirelessly in their respective realms to ensure harmony of the cosmic whole. Their magic is associated with luck, fortune and healing. But cross a fairy and they may turn their magic against you.

Why Contact Fairies?

In earlier times, contacting fairies was not seen as a desirable activity. Fairies were believed to be dangerous and unpredictable, even hostile toward humans. They might kidnap you, bewitch you, play tricks on you or steal your children. Today our attitude has shifted: it is not only desirable but necessary to have an understanding of the beings in the natural landscape and in our homes and machines. In turn, fairies have responded with increased openness to mutually beneficial communication and work.

Knowledge about fairies and the ability to discern them is useful in personal spiritual work and also in paranormal investigations. Fairies that occupy homes may make their presence felt to the occupants in ways similar to ghosts and poltergeists, especially the latter. In lore, fairies are fond of moving objects around, and if they are unhappy they make messes and create disturbances. They can appear and disappear like apparitions. In natural settings, a strong fairy presence can contribute to a "haunted" atmosphere. If you learn how to tune into them, fairies will distinguish themselves from other entities present, and this information will be conveyed to you intuitively.

How Fairies Make Themselves Known

Special psychic gifts aren't necessary to perceive fairies. They show up when you're in harmony with your environment. We often don't notice them because we don't know how to look for them, or we dismiss them as our imagination. They may be right in front of us.

Fairies often make themselves known as sparkling balls of light. Once I lived in a wooded area in Connecticut, and I liked to look out a big picture window into the trees at dusk. During these reveries, I became aware of silvery-white lights that either floated or shot quickly around. I noticed the lights especially at times when I was in a peaceful mood, not thinking of anything in particular, but simply drinking in the beauty, scents, and sounds of the environment around me. On moonlit nights, the woods were magical with lights. I also noticed the lights at dawn.

I discovered that I didn't "see" these lights literally, but rather perceived with my inner eye. If I averted my physical vision and did not look directly into the woods, the lights were more prominent.

I began practicing this averted vision technique in other locations. It worked. Sometimes the lights sparkled like jewels on the ground sort of like the way cities look at night when seen at high altitude from an airplane.

One summer, I heard fairy music for the first time. In lore, fairies love to dance and sing and play musical instruments. That summer I was in Findhorn, Scotland, for a summer solstice festival. Findhorn became famous for its nature spirits, or devas, who communicated in mediumship and told the community members how to tend their gardens and relate to nature in a more spiritual way.

During my stay, I meditated to tune in to the environment. I paid attention to all the elements and felt myself a part of them. At twilight, I could perceive the glowing lights of nature spirits.

I had heard that Pan, the pagan ruler of nature spirits, might make himself known if he approved of you. One day when I was hiking alone to the beach, I suddenly heard behind me the distinct sound of panpipes, Pan's musical flute. At first I thought a person was behind me, but the trail was empty. The music followed me all the way out to the beach. I believe it was Pan saying hello.

On another occasion, I had a distinct mental impression of a fairy who looked like a small person. I was meditating on the roots of a huge oak tree at the ruins of a sacred site, a Roman dream temple in Lydney, England. The tree itself seemed to be a portal between worlds.

After a while, I suddenly became aware that I was being regarded by a small figure who had materialized by the tree, as though he had emerged from the roots. His clothing was not distinct, but I could clearly make out the vivid red cap on his head. He seemed old, like a little old man, and I had the impression of gray whiskers or beard. I guessed his height at about two feet. He seemed curious about me. I knew he wanted me to see him and acknowledge him, for if he had wished to watch me in secrecy he could have easily done so.

I gave him a mental greeting and thanked him for joining me. I received a mental impression of a greeting in return, and his appreciation of my respect for the place. He stayed for a bit, and then suddenly he was gone. I had the impression that he disappeared back down the tree roots. Sometimes fairies just like to drop in and check us out.

Tips for Developing Fairy Sight

You can improve your own ability to perceive fairies by meditating on a regular basis, which expands your consciousness into the unseen realms. Ask the fairies to make themselves known to you. Practice harmony with your environment wherever you go remember, some fairies live indoors, too. On an investigation, tune in to the place and feel yourself centered and relaxed.

Try averting your vision. Fairies often appear in peripheral vision, where they create an impression rather than a distinct visual image. Fairies can be seen at any time, but you may have the best results at transition times such as dusk and dawn. If you receive peripheral impressions and mental messages, don't dismiss them as your imagination.

Cultivating the Fairy Presence

To invite fairies into your home, make a "fairy nook." Fairies are appreciative of special places you set aside for them. It's a sign to them that you are mindful of their well-being and wish them to be a participant in the household.

A household fairy will make known to you where the best place is in your home for a fairy nook. Fairies like places where they can survey rooms, and where they are out of the main household traffic and areas where guests are entertained. Bookshelves and tables in corners and alcoves are favorites.

The presence of iron will send fairies away, for iron saps their strength and repels them. Keep iron objects from areas in your home where you feel a fairy presence. (And do not use iron implements in your garden.)

When you are near their nook, greet the fairies and inquire how they are getting along. You needn't speak out loud, for fairies will pick up on your thoughts.

In addition to a fairy nook, you may wish to set up a fairy altar. Altars are important in spiritual work, for they represent the meeting place of heaven and earth. The altar opens a door to spiritual realms. A fairy altar can serve as both a place to leave gifts for household fairies, and also a place to conduct fairy magic.

Small accent tables and boxes make excellent altars, and can be set up in a corner of your bedroom or a quiet area of the house. If you do not have space for a permanent altar, you can keep your altar objects in a special box and get them out whenever you wish to do a ritual.

Objects for the altar are representatives of the four elements, such as a stone or crystal for earth; a seashell for water; a feather for air; and a candle for fire. You may also wish to add devotional objects related to your spiritual/religious beliefs, lucky charms and things you associate with fairies.

Thankfulness

Above all, give thanks for your experiences fairies love to be appreciated. However, do not leave coins, for many fairies are offended by outright offerings of money. The best way to show appreciation is to take care of your home and respect the natural world. In lore, small bits of food and dishes of cream are the preferred offerings of thanks to the fairies. If they've appeared during one of your investigations, leave a tiny snack behind.

To order additional copies of this book,
please send full amount plus $5.00 for
postage and handling for the first book and
$1.00 for each additional book.
Minnesota residents add 7.125 percent sales tax

Send orders to:

Galde Press
PO Box 460
Lakeville, Minnesota 55044-0460

Credit card orders call 1–800–777–3454
Fax (952) 891–6091
Visit our website at *www.galdepress.com*
and download our free catalog,
or write for our catalog.